Case-Studies
in Adolescence

PAULINE PERRY, M.A.

Tutor in Education
North Berkshire College of Further Education

GEORGE W. PERRY, M.A., B.Sc., M.Ed.

Senior Staff Tutor
University of Oxford Department of Educational Studies

First published 1970

SIR ISAAC PITMAN AND SONS LTD.
Pitman House, Parker Street, Kingsway, London, W.C.2
P.O. Box 6038, Portal Street, Nairobi, Kenya

SIR ISAAC PITMAN (AUST.) PTY. LTD.
Pitman House, Bouverie Street, Carlton, Victoria 3053, Australia

PITMAN PUBLISHING COMPANY S.A. LTD.
P.O. Box 9898, Johannesburg, S. Africa

PITMAN PUBLISHING CORPORATION
6 East 43rd Street, New York, N.Y. 10017, U.S.A.

SIR ISAAC PITMAN (CANADA) LTD.
Pitman House, 381–383 Church Street, Toronto, 3, Canada

THE COPP CLARK PUBLISHING COMPANY
517 Wellington Street, Toronto, 2B, Canada

SBN: 273 40709 0

Made in Great Britain at the Pitman Press, Bath
G0—(G.4614)

Contents

Introductory

These cases are stories from the life of real adolescents, each one based on a true incident, as told to us by some of the young people involved themselves.

We have studiously avoided any kind of adult judgement anywhere in the telling of the stories, and any judgements which seem to be passed are those of the young people who told us the stories. From amongst the very large number of stories and cases that we have collected in the course of case-study work with adolescents, this selection attempts to present a representative picture of those problems and questions which the pupils and students themselves named as of greatest concern to them.

The cases here are about people who have in common their age—they are all between the ages of fourteen and nineteen—yet the more one works with people of this age-group, from a multiplicity of backgrounds and experience, the more one realizes that the problems which unite them are greater than those which divide. The concern of the boy who looks for the right apprenticeship at fifteen has much in common with the concern of the eighteen-year-old girl who looks for guidance in choosing between marriage and a career. Shyness with the opposite sex, frustration and affection in conflicting doses as one contemplates one's parents—these are common to the age-group, not the pre-rogative of any one "type" of background or educational level.

I

The cases are evenly divided between those seen through the eyes of boys and those through the eyes of girls. The setting of the stories varies from home to school, to youth-club or workshop. While we have divided the cases, in the index at the front of the book, under topic headings, these headings are to a large extent rather superficial, since no problem or event in real life can be exactly put into a single category. These cases are slices of real lives, and as such they contain a network of relationships involving parents, teachers, youth-club leaders, probation workers, sisters and brothers, boy-friends and girl-friends, and so on.

Finally, we would emphasize again that these stories are told as they were told to us—that is, they are as seen by the young people directly involved in the events. The adults in the stories are, to a major extent, adults as seen by adolescents, and the tolerance and sympathy they express for us as adults has been one of the most moving parts of the task of collecting these cases.

Because of the insight offered into the thinking of adolescents which their own way of telling a story has given to us, we have preserved as far as possible this quality, to make the book valuable to teachers and youth-workers, both in training and in service. After several sessions of discussing similar case-studies, the pupils and students with whom we worked were invited to write a story from their own individual first-hand experience. They wrote these freely and anonymously, so that what emerged was a very frank and full picture of their major concerns, within the lens of their private viewpoint.

All of the cases are, of course, completely disguised to save any embarrassment on the part of the originals themselves. In terms of the relationships and emotions they portray, however, they are, as nearly as possible, an exact representation of the characters' own vision of people and events.

For teachers in Humanities, Social Studies, and Liberal Studies, the approach of the case-study has begun to prove one of the most fruitful methods of sparking discussion about questions which are close to the lives of the young people they teach, but perhaps too close to make the broaching of the subject an easy matter.

Case-studies are, for young people, a way into objective discussion of their biggest problems—problems of into-work decisions, family conflicts, sexual relationships and morality, and the reasons which lead some of their number into delinquency. In discussing and sharing their thoughts under a teacher's guidance, young people may accomplish two major steps towards maturity. Firstly, they may begin to realize that their problems are not unique—that others of their age wrestle with the same problems—and secondly, they begin to see that the other people, perhaps of different generations, with whom they interact, also have deep feelings and problems.

The aim, then, in using case-studies in adolescence with adolescents, is above all to achieve objective insight into their own and other people's feelings and behaviour. A further outcome of the use of the studies with discussion is that the force of group decision begins to operate, over some of the issues brought out by the case-study. Should a boy see a girl home after a date? Should he meet her parents first? As the group discuss these questions, their opinions begin to emerge, and the standards of behaviour for each as an individual are set by the group's high standards for itself. No-one, after all, likes to admit publicly that his or her standards are lower than the average!

In using case-studies with a class, we would suggest introducing a study fresh at the beginning of a lesson, so that the material is still new to the pupils. Their natural wish to discuss the behaviour of their peers in the story can lead to immediately lively discussion. Some of these studies have been used with boys and girls who were either totally or semi-illiterate, and for these, it is obviously better to read the case-study aloud, or to tape it previously.

We would suggest that the first discussion, possibly lasting fifteen to twenty minutes—less on the first few occasions of using cases—should be held amongst very small groups, of only five or so pupils. This enables each pupil to take an active part in the early discussion, and to make any inferences about their own immediate experience which arise from the story. No-one need discourage the sort of reminiscence which is frequently sparked off after the first few minutes of comment on the characters in the story. Indeed, a great deal of helpful free discussion can arise from pupils or students remembering similar cases from their own experience.

There seems to be little use for the "set" questions at this stage—few groups are incapable of lively thought about a case without guidance. General suggestions, if any are needed, should be used at first, rather than specific questions. We have kept to vague directions such as "What do you think about this story?" or, "Why do you think this happened?"

When the groups seem to have exhausted their own resources, the time has come for the class as a whole to compare notes on what they have decided or felt about the case. This is the time when the teacher can raise very general issues arising from the case. Topics of loyalty, family conflicts, worries about examinations, violence, drugs, sexual morality—as these seem to have arisen in the earlier small-group discussion, so the wise teacher can direct the class out of the specifics of the characters in the case-study, and their actions, into the general issues facing the pupils and students themselves.

Further work, to find out, for instance, the facts on drug-addiction, or the facts about teenage marriage, can arise as

4

teacher and class feel the need. Sometimes the early discussion is so intense and meaningful that the teacher may feel enough has been accomplished at that stage. At other times, the work which follows may be the most useful part of the exercise—certainly, the tone of the discussion about a case-study can provide an excellent guide to the teacher as to where the interest of the class truly lies.

Sometimes, it may be helpful to vary the ways in which thoughts from the small-group discussion are shared between the whole class and teacher. Role-playing of "How would you deal with this incident?"—where each group provides a demonstration role-play for the other groups, of their way of behaving in the situation which faced some character from the case study—this can be a very valuable way of trying out behaviour which still seems difficult or worrying to young people.

The questions at the end of each case-study are intended as guides for the teacher, rather than for class use. These questions can sometimes be useful for a final drawing-together of thoughts about the case, at the end of discussion, but no-one need feel that they are a necessary or comprehensive list of all the subjects that arise from the class. Many of our colleagues, like ourselves, have been most pleasantly surprised and instructed by the issues which a case contains for young people. These may, or may not, bear any relationship to the issues it seems to have for us.

Case-studies in adolescence have great value, as we have said earlier, for those who are working, or training to work, with young people of this age-group. With students and groups of this kind of adult, of course, the discussion will take a quite different turn, and we need hardly add that the questions at the end of the cases will not be relevant. Adults will be more concerned with the behaviour of the adults in the case—or, indeed, the lack of any evidence of adult interest, which is sometimes the lesson for us to learn from the way young people see our relevance to some of their problems!

Many of these cases are difficult ones for adults—often there is evidence of a breakdown in communication between adult and young person, and it is useful to spend some thought on the problem of how one could, so to speak, "do better" if this kind of problem were to come our way.

It is not possible to over-emphasize the importance of a teacher being as un-authoritarian as possible in the discussions which follow case-studies. The value of this kind of discussion is that it is a way in which young people may reach their own agreed standards of behaviour, and decide on their own values, appropriate to their own generation and time. Many of the major issues of our human condition in this century are issues on which there is no consensus in adult society, and therefore no consensus as to the teacher's message to young people. The teacher's job is to open the issues to free, intelligent discussion, and to provide the facts as and where they are appropriate. After that, it is also the teacher's job to allow each young person to come to conclusions based upon their life experience, their position in society and in the generations.

Mary and her Mother

Mary was the second of three daughters. Hers was a happy family, by and large, although Mary and her mother fought continually, over quite small things.

Mary was considered by her parents and teachers in Primary School to be the bright member of the family. Her older sister had not passed the eleven plus, but Mary was told that if she worked hard enough she would pass, and be able to go to the Grammar School. More than anything else, Mary just wanted to please her father, whom she adored. He always made a great fuss of her, and called her "His little girl." She asked him if he would be pleased if she went to the Grammar School, and he just laughed, and said that whatever she did was all right with him.

When the results of the eleven plus examination came through, Mary had been given a place at the secondary modern school. Both her parents said how terribly disappointed they were, and seemed to think that she had not really tried hard enough. Mary decided that she didn't care one way or the other—she had found a great interest in Domestic Science, and she determined to get enough "O" levels to train as a demonstrator. She settled down well in her new school, worked well, and had three happy years there.

During the Easter holidays of Mary's third year at school, her parents moved house, in the same town, but to a totally different area. This meant that Mary had to transfer to a different school. She fought against the whole idea, and had many arguments with her parents, blaming them for moving at this time. They became very impatient with her, and told her she was just making a great fuss over nothing.

Mary spent less than two years at the new school, hating every single minute of the time. She never got into any serious trouble with the teachers, but her reports were poor, and she failed to make any real friends amongst the girls. She was just too far away from her old friends to keep up any really close contact, and she found that when she did meet them she no longer felt a part of the old group.

Just before her fifteenth birthday, she went to each of her parents in turn, and told them that she didn't like school, and asked what they thought she should do. Should she leave school and get a job right away from home, perhaps in London? Her mother said flatly, "I'm not going to give you any advice, you'll have to make up your own mind.

I know you only too well—if my advice turned out wrong I'd never hear the end of whose fault it was."

Mary turned to her father next, but he just said, "It's up to you, little girl, do whatever will make you happy." He raised no objection when she wrote off for an interview for a job in London, as a trainee punch-card operator.

Mary got the job, and astonished her school friends by telling them that she was leaving school, and going to live in London, sharing a flat with another, older girl whom she had known at school. Mary had been a quiet, stay-at-home sort of girl for so long that her teachers expressed doubts as to whether she had made the right decision. Against the advice of friends and teachers alike, however, Mary went off to London and started her job.

Mary came home to visit her parents every three weeks, at week-ends, and seemed to be enjoying her work, and her life in London. She did admit that she found her flat-mate, Susan, difficult to get on with, and indeed, they quarrelled a great deal. On one occasion, Susan wrote to Mary's parents, telling them that Mary had been stealing her possessions, and that she was a constant thief. The two parents ignored the letter, and although her mother showed it to her the next week-end Mary offered no comment, and it was not mentioned again.

After a year, Mary moved out of the flat into a single bed-sitter, and at the same time she changed her job to one in a computer firm. She had been with this firm only two months, when she was caught stealing money from another employee. She was dismissed, and the police were called into the affair. Only then did Mary's parents learn that this was in fact her second offence—she had been caught shop-lifting seven months previously. Mary was put on probation, on condition that she returned home to live with her parents.

Mary's mother was genuinely heart-broken at the way things had turned out for Mary, and obviously determined to do better for her in the future. Although Mary recognized that her mother was deeply upset, she found that the constant watching and suspicion which her mother showed towards her was just more than she could bear. For several months, she tried to get along better at home, and avoid arguments with her mother, but in the end she felt that it was impossible to live with her family any more.

One evening, six months after her return from London, she told the entire family that she had applied to Australia House to emigrate as soon as she was released from probation. Both her parents listened to her explanations, which were fairly calm, and both of them replied that they thought that her ideas were good, and that emigrating to another country might be the best thing. Mary looked from one to the other in total disbelief at their reply, and burst into hysterical sobs and tears. "It's just what I've always known," she said, "You've never really cared about me at all."

Questions for Discussion

1 Why did Mary not get a place at the Grammar School, as her teachers had expected?

2 How terrible is it to move from one school to another when you are fourteen?

3 Were Mary's parents wise to refuse to advise her about her future?

4 What problems do you think are likely to arise for a quiet fifteen-year-old, when she goes to live in London from a small town?

5 Why had Mary been stealing regularly, since she went to live in London?

6 What do you think is wrong with Mary's relationships with her family?

7 Where could Mary have turned, throughout the story, to get better advice and guidance than she seems to have found at home?

The Boy who ran away

Bob was the elder of two boys in the Jennings family. At fifteen, he was a slim, good-looking lad with fair hair curling over his collar. At school, he had the reputation of being "one of the lads." He was frequently in trouble for minor misdemeanours. He had been sent to the Head for smoking, continual lateness and failure to hand in homework on time. Despite this, he managed to maintain a form position around the half-way line, and most teachers were agreed that if only he would spend as much energy on his work as apparently he did on getting into trouble he could easily lead his class. His termly reports for the past two years had monotonously affirmed that he "could do much better," should "work harder," and, more recently, that he was "lazy," "sloppy," and that he "lacked a sense of responsibility."

It was this latter comment which had apparently been the last straw for Bob's father. Mr Jennings was constantly saying that he was a "self-made" man. He had pulled himself up from nothing. In 1945, as a transport sergeant, he had left the Air Force with his gratuity and savings and little else other than the absolute determination never to work for another boss in his life. He had opened his road haulage business with an old War Surplus three-tonner and a small pick-up van, and in the first ten years his only holiday had been a short few days' honeymoon when he had married his secretary. Mr. Jennings felt that he had done fairly well for his family. He owned a large modern house in a select neighbourhood of the town, drove a Rover to the office each day, and kept a boat moored at a South-coast yard. He was a Mason, a member of the County Golf Club and an active Rotarian. His wife was a keen Bridge Club member, and now that all the boys were at school was able to spend a fair amount of time in social work with the W.V.S. and the Red Cross.

In the light of all this, his elder son seemed his only failure. There had seemed so much potential there in the beginning, and probably there still was if only Bob would do something with himself. Sometimes, Mr. Jennings blamed himself because he'd been away so much during the early years. Sometimes, he blamed his wife who obviously had been over-protective with all the children. Perhaps, on the other hand, it was just some throwback, some inherited weakness, perhaps from Mr. Jennings's own father. Whatever it was, Mr. Jennings decided that the time had come for direct strong action. He waved the latest report in front of Bob's face.

"This is enough," he shouted. "Your mother and I have both had enough of your lazy ways. I've told you till I'm blue in the face that this had to change, and now I'm finished talking."

Bob's eyes didn't meet those of his father. He stared silently at the floor; only his flushed face and ears indicated that he was feeling anything.

"All right!" stormed his father. "I'll show you now. I'm cutting your pocket money until the next report. And if that isn't good enough I'll cut it until the next one. One more thing," and he banged the table. "If you don't improve this year, you're out. D'you understand? You're out. I'll not keep a lazy slob just to fool around at school."

Whatever Bob actually felt about his father's outburst he said nothing to the rest of his family. He went to school quite normally and returned at night more or less on time, usually to shut himself in his room after dinner. This, ostensibly, was to do homework, but whenever his brother or his mother went in he was usually lying on his bed reading. Mr. Jennings was immersed in business and until the following weekend was hardly at home. It was not until that Saturday evening that relationships between Bob and his father came to a head again.

There was a small skirmish between them during the afternoon. After lunch Bob had said that he was going over to see a friend. On most Saturday afternoons this announcement would hardly have raised a comment in the Jennings household, but this afternoon Mr. Jennings particularly wanted to get some tidying done in the garden and he had been relying upon Bob for some help with the lawn. A request that Bob might give him a hand for an hour was met only with silence.

"The trouble with you, my lad, is you're bone idle. You'd rather play records all day than do an hour's work," said his father. Bob shrugged his shoulders. "And don't play sulks with me, either. Look at yourself. Even your hair's like a girl. Why the hell don't you get yourself to the barber's sometime?" Bob flushed.

"I'd like to help you. But I can't. I promised Edwards I'd see him this afternoon. I'm sorry . . ." Bob trailed off into silence.

"I'll bet you're sorry," snapped Mr. Jennings. "I'll bet you are." And he stamped off towards the tool shed.

Bob was late getting back, and the meal was half over.

"Where the hell have you been?" demanded Mr. Jennings.

"Just over to Edwards. We were playing records and I didn't notice the time."

"That's just it. You go into a dream and you notice nothing. Records. That's about it. It's all you're fit for," and Mr. Jennings swore. Bob went red, but said nothing. His silence seemed to goad Mr. Jennings into even greater fury. "You're just good for nothing. Well, we're not feeding you if you haven't even the good manners to get home on time. Get to your room. Get out of my sight."

At this point, Mr. Jennings was yelling. Bob looked at him, then looked at his mother who was staring nervously at both of them. "I'm sorry," said Bob lamely. He was hungry, but he knew that there was little use in arguing.

He went to his room and threw himself on his bed. He felt churned up inside.

Downstairs, all was not well with the Jennings parents.

"It's no use just losing your temper," said Mrs. Jennings. "You should have let the boy have something to eat and punished him in another way."

"I should have done what I should have done years ago," said Mr. Jennings. "A good hiding would do him the world of good." Just then the sound of the latest pop hit came through from Bob's room. "You see!" shouted Mr. Jennings. "You see!" and he ran up to his son's room. He threw open the door.

"Take that damn thing off. D'you hear me. Take it off or I will." He seized Bob by the collar and threw him towards the record player. "Take it off, I tell you." Father and son faced one another. Mr. Jennings was shaking.

"Take it off yourself," said Bob. Mr. Jennings's hand flew out to Bob's face. He hit his son, hard. For some seconds there was absolute silence, then Bob moved past his father and ran down the stairs and out of the house. He was trying not to cry as he went.

He walked to the end of the road, wondering what he should do. At last he went over to the Edwards' house, hoping that his friend John would still be in, although he knew Mr. and Mrs. Edwards were going out. John let him in.

"I'm not going back there," said Bob. "Nobody wants me. I'm better out of it."

John was sympathetic, but he had no suggestions as to what Bob should do. "I can lend you ten bob if it's any good to you, but you can't stay here."

"I'll think I'll go to Newtown. Wilcocks may help me. He's just had a new summerhouse built in his garden. Perhaps I can stay there for the night. If not, then there's Charters's place. Didn't he say his parents were away for the week-end?"

Bob left his friend an hour later, complete with a bag of sandwiches and John's ten-shillings, and headed for Newtown.

In the meantime, at Bob's home, Mr. Jennings had retired to the television set. The ten o'clock news appeared, and still Bob had not returned. Mrs. Jennings was, by this time, quite frantic with anxiety. "You must do something. You must. If only you hadn't lost your temper!"

Mr. Jennings, however, was still angry. "He'll come home all right. And just wait till he does."

Eleven o'clock came. Still no Bob. Mr. Jennings, now seething, picked up the phone and called the Edwards. Mr. Edwards answered. No, he hadn't seen Bob since that afternoon, but he would ask his son.

John Edwards finally came on the phone. "Yes, Mr. Jennings, Bob was here, but he went some time ago. I don't know where."

"What about his other friends?" said Mr. Jennings.

"Well, perhaps," said John, after a pause. "You could try Spooner and Evans. They might know." He didn't mention either Wilcocks or Charters. He felt very loyal to his friend Bob as he put the phone down. He hadn't even mentioned the phone numbers of either Spooner or Evans either. Let the stupid old so-and-so find his own numbers.

Next morning, John phoned Charters. "Yes, he's here," said Charters. "But my old man and woman are away until Wednesday so that Jennings can stay here until then. After that we'll have to think again. But he's not going back to that place, that's for certain. Why don't you get over when you can? We're going to have a party."

Questions for Discussion

1 What could have been some of the reasons for Bob Jennings doing so badly at school?

2 Do you think that Bob's father behaved correctly? If you were Bob's father, how would you behave if you found that your son was doing badly at school?

3 What are the sorts of things children help their parents with at secondary school age?

4 If you had been Bob, how would you have reacted over the supper and record incidents?

5 How do you think Mrs. Jennings behaved during all this?

6 What do you think about the loyalty of Edwards and Charters towards their friend Bob?

7 What do you think Bob should do now that he has run away from home?

8 If you were in Bob's parents' place, what would you do if your son failed to return home after he had had a row with you?

9 Imagine that Bob has finally come home after a week-end away. Develop a role-play to show how you think the difficulties in the situation could be worked out.

Child of Divorce

When Sally was still a little girl, in Primary School, her parents had told her that they were going to get a divorce. As she was only eight at the time, Sally had great trouble understanding what it would all mean, but her parents had made a real effort to help her to understand, and particularly to make her realize that they both loved her.

From as long ago as she could remember, Sally had heard her parents fighting with each other, and her mother fighting with her grandmother, her father's mother. These fights had upset Sally all the time, and when her parents first explained to her that they were not going to live together any more, Sally had said, "That means you won't fight each other any more, then."

Only as she began to understand that "divorce" meant, too, that she was going away from her father, and would not see very much of him, did Sally really know that this was a bad thing that was happening. She loved both her parents very much, and it seemed to her very strange that they could not also love each other.

When she grew older, Sally could list to herself the various incidents which made the whole period of her parents' divorce such an unexpected nightmare for a girl of eight. First was the break from her home, and all the familiar things of her neighbourhood. It was her mother who was leaving her father, to live with another man, and her father had agreed to let Sally remain with her mother. Sally's mother explained to her that she loved this man, and wanted Sally to love him as well. Sally, however, hated the man, and the caravan in which she had to live with him and her mother. She was desperately homesick, and missed her father very much.

From time to time, Sally went to spend week-ends with her father, at her old home, which was very close to the caravan site. Her father seemed delighted to have her with him, and she used to beg him to let her stay with him. She told him how she hated the caravan, but he reminded her that she would miss her mother if she came to live with him, and explained to her that he didn't know how to look after little girls—they needed a Mummy for all the details of their lives.

The worst part of the whole affair, though, came when the divorce proceedings became public, and everyone realized that her parents were getting a divorce. Neighbours and casual acquaintances seemed to regard Sally as a sort of unofficial and unfeeling source to be pumped for all news and details of gossip. People she hardly knew stopped her in the street to ask for information, and question her as to whether she liked her "new Daddy." Her teacher at school was the worst of all, though. She kept taking Sally aside for little private talks, saying how happy she must be that it had all ended at last, and wasn't she lucky to have it all work out so well?

Sally bore all this in stubborn silence, learning how to give nothing away, and only speaking to contradict anyone who seemed to indicate that her father was in any way to blame, or that she was glad to be away from him.

This period lasted for two years—until it was time for Sally to leave her Junior school. Although her parents' divorce had come through, her mother never married the man Sally disliked, and for a year or so she and her mother had lived alone in a miserable one-roomed flat. When Sally was twelve her mother married again—a very nice man, who had a lovely home, and who showered presents on Sally and made her mother happier than she had ever been before, at least in Sally's memory.

For the first time in many years, Sally found herself beginning to feel at school that she had a normal home-life that she could talk about. She loved to show her friends the gifts her step-father had bought for her, and she did not realize that they thought she was showing off. She still went to see her father often, and now he, too, began to buy her expensive presents, and sometimes he would beg her not to forget him. This made Sally feel just dreadful—she felt that it was disloyal to her father even to like her step-father, and she would try very hard to be distant and cool when she got back home.

After her week-ends with her father, her step-father would question Sally about what had happened, and try to criticize her father to her. He even tried to tell her that the divorce had all been her father's fault, a subject which Sally had refused to discuss for years. Her step-father asked her several times if she didn't love him better than her father, and this just made her think what a stupid man he must be.

Once again, Sally found that she was deeply unhappy and confused in spite of her nice home and all her possessions. Even her school friends seemed to have turned against her. They didn't seem interested in anything she had to say, and her worries were not subjects she wanted to discuss with anyone. Her friends told her, one day, in the middle of an argument, that she had become really selfish, always wanting things her own way, and they were tired of it.

When her father announced that he was going to marry again, Sally was fourteen. She met his new wife, and tried to be a bit pleasant, as she felt that this woman might refuse to let her see her father if she didn't like her, and by now Sally was quite sure that there were few people in the world who liked her. She went to her father's wedding, but refused to go to the reception afterwards, as people started asking her questions about "her new Mummy," and she felt too terribly tired to parry the questions any longer.

As the first few months of her father's new marriage went by Sally became more and more unhappy. She found herself getting into arguments with her mother, and yet when she went to seek comfort in her father's home, she no longer felt really welcome there. She disliked his wife and found it too much of an effort to try to be polite to her. Her step-mother confided in her that she was expecting a baby at the end of the year, and Sally tried to decide how she felt about this news.

One month exactly after Sally's fifteenth birthday, she had a new half-sister. Going over to visit her father, and seeing his absolute delight in the new baby, and his love for his wife, seemed to Sally like the last straw. She felt she hated the new baby, belonged to no-one in the world, and wondered why she had ever been born.

Questions for Discussion

1 Do you think Sally might have grown up better if her parents had stayed together, in spite of their quarrels?

18

2 What is the kindest way for friends to behave, when a child is involved in something like divorce proceedings?

3 How do you think Sally's early experiences affected her personality?

4 Is there any way anyone could have acted to make Sally's relationship with her step-father more successful?

5 Why had Sally become so selfish in her behaviour with her friends?

6 Are Sally's feelings towards her step-mother quite natural? How could their relationship be improved?

7 What could be done now, to help Sally, and show her how to be happy again?

Three Sisters

Daphne will tell you that being the eldest of three sisters is just about the worst position in the family that anyone could have.

Daphne is fifteen, and her younger sisters are twelve and seven. She is very fond of Marianne, her youngest sister, but finds Mary, the twelve-year-old, more than she can bear. Even her relationship with Marianne is ruined by Mary, who never notices the littlest sister for weeks on end, and then suddenly rushes in with some present or sweets to spoil her completely.

The mother of the three girls, Mrs. Rogers, considers Daphne to be the best daughter any mother could have. Sometimes, when Mr. Rogers would tease Daphne, who was rather fat, Mrs. Rogers would just laugh and say, "Never mind if Daphne is the one who never marries—she'll stay home and look after her Mother always, won't you, dear?"

Daphne felt rather disloyal at her irritation with this particular remark of her mother's. She adored her mother, and frequently felt quite fiercely that her father did not appreciate her mother enough. She used to dream of how she would make lots of money when she grew up, and buy wonderful things for her mother—a big house, with expensive gadgets in the kitchen, and so on.

Certainly, the whole Rogers family seemed to rely on Daphne for a great deal of its day-to-day smooth running. Young as she had been, when Marianne was born Daphne had looked after her father and Mary while her mother was in hospital, and she had helped enormously, too, when her mother came home—even hanging out the nappies in the morning before she went off to school. She was extremely helpful around the house, and Mrs. Rogers had got into the habit of leaving a great many routine jobs for Daphne to do when she came home from school in the evenings.

Sometimes friends would comment on the amount of work Daphne did in the house compared to her sister Mary. Daphne always answered angrily when she overheard this remark, for she believed it to be a criticism of her mother.

"Mary has her homework to do," she would explain—(Mary was at the Grammar School, whereas Daphne was at the Secondary Modern School)—"And anyway, I like housework. I'm good at it, and Mary is hopeless."

Marianne seemed in many ways to regard Daphne as her mother, just as much as her real mother. She would shout out for Daphne to come and see her, long after she had gone to bed, claiming that she was "frightened," or that the light was too bright, or not bright enough. Some nights she would insist that Daphne stay with her until she went to sleep, and this Daphne did without complaint.

Just occasionally, Daphne asks herself whether her constant fighting with Mary comes from her own jealousy. Mary is pretty, slim, clever—everything that Daphne is not. On the other hand, Daphne likes her own school, and is unquestionably her mother's favourite, and this, she is sure, more than makes up for everything else. Why, then, does she so often feel miserable? Why these dreadful, constant rows with Mary over silly little details, like whose nylons Mary is wearing, or the mess that Mary makes over Daphne's side of the room, as well as her own?

The times when she finds Mary really hardest to take are when Mary teases, especially when she joins with their father in front of Marianne to tease Daphne. The worst time had been at tea-time the other day. Daphne had been trying, not for the first time, to follow a diet for weight-reducing. Mary heard Marianne echo Daphne's refusal of a piece of cake, and immediately she moved into the fray.

"Don't tell me you're going on a diet, kid!" she laughed. "You're a pretty little girl, all the boys like you. You don't have to worry. Take it from an expert—eating cake will make you clever, and you'd like that, wouldn't you?"

She plonked the cake on to Marianne's plate, and giggled as Marianne looked doubtfully at her. "Look at Daphne, then, going without cake hasn't done much for her, has it? A few more diets and we'll have to make a bigger hole for the doorway, just to get her in at night."

Daphne intended to smile good-humouredly—her mother always said no-one minded fat people as long as they could laugh at themselves—but Marianne's giggles suddenly seemed more than she could take. She had burst out in fury, saying quite unforgivable things to Mary, calling her a snob. She was goaded still more, stupid as it was, when she realized that she was frightening Marianne by her uncontrolled display of violent temper.

Her father had tried to calm her down, by asking her what had happened to her sense of humour, and even her mother had said "Mary was only teasing, dear." Finally she had run from the room in tears, and cried in her room for what seemed hours. When Mary came up to do her homework, she went back downstairs and helped with the washing-up, in the hope that her mother would at least be grateful, and forgive her the outburst.

The worst part about it all was that everyone seemed to have forgotten the whole incident, except for Marianne, who seemed to regard her with slight fear or caution for several days.

Questions for Discussion

1 What do you think is the worst position in the family?

2 Does Daphne's own attitude account for her feeling of not being happy?

3 Is there anything Daphne could do that would stop people making fun of her?

4 What does Daphne do to make people love her? Is this a good way?

5 Is it true that girls who have homework don't need to help in the house as much as those who have very little school work at night?

6 What sort of person is Mary? Do you think she is to blame for Daphne's unhappiness?

7 Why was Daphne so upset by the last incident at tea-time?

The Attack on the Girl

There were three of them, Jocko, Ginger, and Whitey. They'd been through the same primary school, and when they were in their third year of secondary school, had some-how gravitated together. Now, in their last year at school, they seemed an inseparable trio. None of them was much of a scholar. Ginger and Jocko could barely read, and when-ever it was necessary to get anything out of a book in class they usually relied upon their friend Whitey, who was the accepted "brain" among the three of them. If one of them got into trouble, then all three were in trouble, and as one of them was invariably discovered up to something, then their visits to the Head or his Deputy were fairly frequent. In fact, as a trio they were becoming notorious with all members of staff, although at least so far they had managed to keep out of Juvenile court. The Head was a humane màn, and had always hated using a cane, although he had to admit that sometimes it was the only thing that seemed to have any real effect. He had to have the trio in only the week before, and now here they were again with a charge against them which this time sounded really serious.

The three boys were far from happy. Most of that afternoon they had spent with the Deputy, telling their stories separately over and over again. Even to Jock, it was obvious that the Deputy didn't believe them.

It had all started after dinner that day. Whitey had a packet of cigarettes, and the three of them decided to have a quiet smoke behind the old tool shed at the far end of the school garden. Normally, the school garden was out-of-bounds to all pupils unless they were working there, and although it wasn't possible to go through the gate being spotted by the teacher-on-duty or a prefect, any boy—or girl for that matter—could get in without being seen if they went through the fence at the bottom of the garden where it met the playing field in one corner.

Normally, it was a fairly quiet place, and although if you were caught you were punished, a secretly smoked cigarette, according to the trio, was well worth the risk. On this occasion, they had just lit up, their backs resting comfortably against the warm wood of the old shed, when they heard the sound of girls' voices. The three boys "froze." They distrusted girls at the best of times, and these could be prefects, in which case they would certainly be for it.

The girls came to the shed and opened the door. From the way they were talking and the sounds of tools being moved, they were obviously looking for something.

"Mr. Jones swore he'd left it here, Sally. It must be here somewhere. Oh, do look for it."

The boys wondered what "it" was. Obviously, they had been sent there by a master, and they were probably prefects. Jocko, a little belatedly, was trying to stub out the cigarette in the soil without making any noise, but winced slightly when the burning end caught his fingers.

The girls came out of the shed, and for the three boys the worst happened. "Perhaps he left it round the back, Jackie. Let's look." And almost immediately, there were the two girls, looking very startled at the sight of the boys. "Ooh!" said Susan.

The boys felt suddenly very silly sitting there. Jocko guffawed, and tried to light the dead cigarette again. The girls weren't prefects after all. Just a couple from the fourth form, one of whom, Jackie, went around with an older lad who lived only a few doors from Whitey. Ginger was the first on his feet.

"You're not going to tell on us, are you?" he said.

The girls shook their heads. The boys had a reputation for getting really nasty when they wanted to. "We only came looking for Mr. Jones' tobacco pouch, that's all."

"I'll bet they'll tell," said Jocko. "They're bound to. They're just a couple of stupid birds."

"We won't, honestly we won't."

"You will. We know your lot."

"No, honestly."

The girls were pleading, and Jocko at least began to feel master of the situation. He was beginning to enjoy himself.

"I don't——believe you," he said, and he caught the smaller girl, Susan, by the arm. "You know what we do to kids who split on us, don't you?" and he whispered in her ear.

"No, you wouldn't," Susan said. She was trying not to cry.

"Oh, leave her alone, Jocko. It'll only make it worse if you make her cry," said Whitey.

"Why should I leave her alone? She spoiled our smoke, didn't she? Little tart." He twisted her arm and pushed her against the wall of the shed. "I'll do more than that to you!"

Susan was crying.

"Oh, leave her alone, you big slob. Leave her alone, will you!" and Jackie tried to pull him away. He turned savagely on the girl, and the next moment both of them were rolling and struggling on the ground. Then suddenly her head cracked against the corner of the shed, and for a second she lay still with Jocko on top of her. Susan half-screamed, and with her hand on her mouth ran down the path towards the school.

"Lay off, Jocko. Lay off. They won't tell. They've had enough," and his two friends pulled Jocko to his feet. Jackie was still lying there, her face white, a small trickle of blood coming from behind her ear. Her blouse was torn at the waist, and her short mini-skirt rucked up. She'd begun to cry in hard, dry spasms.

"Go on," said Whitey to the girl. "You'll be O.K. Jocko didn't mean it. Honest, he didn't." Jackie sat up slowly, still crying. Whitey helped her to her feet. "Honestly, it was an accident." She turned away, sobbing, and went up the path towards the school.

"You stupid oaf, Jocko. Now you've really gone and done it," Jocko seemed hardly to hear. He was still panting from the struggle on the ground, and kept muttering to himself, "Stupid bitch, stupid little tart."

The three boys made their way back to the main school and were met on the playing field by the master-on-duty, who looked very stern and hard.

"You again, White? And you other two? You'll land in gaol yet, all three of you. The Deputy wants you. Get going, smartly. Go on, run, you lazy good-for-nothings."

The next hour was the worst grilling that any of the trio could remember. Despite Jocko, they'd tried to get their story

25

straight before they met the master-on-duty. They weren't smoking. They'd gone to finish some weeding. Yes, they knew they should have asked permission, but they couldn't find Mr. Harris, the rural science teacher. When the girls came they were just larking about and Jackie fell and hit her head. But the Deputy was an old hand. If they weren't smoking, whose was the cigarette butt he had found on the ground? And how was it the cigarette was the same as those in White's pockets? And why did White have any cigarettes anyhow? Didn't they know it was against school rules to bring cigarettes to school?

The three boys knew that the Deputy had them. White, of all people, knew when he was beaten. He was brought back into the Deputy's room alone. The Deputy was staring out of the window and was ominously silent.

"Well?" he said, at last. White remained quiet.

"This is a fine mess you're in now. You'd better tell me the truth now and get it over with. I want to know what happened behind that shed this lunch hour." The Deputy glared at him.

"Well, we were smoking, sir, and these two girls came up."

"And?" said the Deputy.

"That's all, sir, really sir." The Deputy looked at him as though he was something that had crawled out from under a stone.

"We were just fooling around, that's all, sir, really." Whitey was whimpering a little. "We didn't do anything. Honestly."

The Deputy looked out of the window, then at Whitey. "Don't give me that story, White. I know very well what you did. I want the truth out of you, if we have to stay here all afternoon. The truth, d'you hear me?"

Whitey knew it was no good. "Well, sir, it was an accident, really. She just slipped. That's all."

"Some accident, White." He was looking very grim. In

all the time Whitey had known him, he had never looked so grim. He couldn't think what had happened to make it all like this. Perhaps Jackie had passed out again. But not even that . . . and Whitey stopped his thoughts from wandering.

"Some accident. I tell you I know what happened, White. And you're going to tell me."

"I've told you, sir. Really, I have."

"You've told me nothing, White, except a pack of lies from start to finish. Now you tell me how you and your pals assaulted this girl. Go on, I'm listening."

Assault. Whitey had heard the word and he knew roughly what it meant. He knew it was bad, much worse than just fooling around. What had happened to the girl? Something awful, that was obvious. He searched for words that wouldn't let his mates down. "We didn't, sir, I swear we didn't."

The Deputy was very angry. "Don't talk about swearing to me. You assaulted her and you know you did. But you did worse than that, didn't you? This wasn't ordinary assault, White. This was indecent assault. And by Harry, we'll prove it!"

Whitey felt himself go cold inside. He knew only imperfectly what the Deputy was saying, but he knew it was about as bad as it could be. Jocko couldn't have. They hadn't. He knew they hadn't.

"Right," said the Deputy, now very quiet again. "You've lied enough to me. Now let's see what story you have to tell to the Headmaster. For all your sakes it had better be the right one."

Questions for Discussion

1 How would you rate boys like Jocko, Ginger and Whitey?

2 "Birds of a feather flock together." Do you think that boys like the three in the case study are the kind who will go

on being friends? How far do you think their feelings of loyalty towards one another are likely to go?

3 Boys like Jocko, Ginger and Whitey are bound to distrust girls. How far do you think that this statement is true?

4 In the circumstances, what do you think of the behaviour of the girls both during and after the incident behind the gardening shed?

5 If you had discovered three boys like this, obviously breaking certain school rules, what would you do?

6 How far should ordinary citizens actively attempt to uphold the law when they see that it is being broken and that interference will involve personal risk for themselves? Are there any circumstances when the ordinary individual should definitely interfere, regardless of consequences? Are there circumstances in which it is better to "stay quiet"?

7 Suppose you had been in Whitey's position. How would you have behaved when questioned by the Deputy Head?

8 Suppose you had been the Deputy Head. What action would you have taken with the three boys on hearing about the incident behind the gardening shed?

9 Imagine that you were involved in the kind of scuffle behind the gardening shed that did occur, and that the girls have just left. What would you do now? Develop a small role-play to show how you might behave.

10 If you had been the girls involved in the incident, what would you have done when you returned to the school building? Work out a small role-play to show your actions.

Joey the Clown

Young Joe Morgan's future was quite clear. He was going to be a clown. Not that this was Joe's choice, or for that matter, even in his mind, but all his teachers predicted it, as did most of the form to which he belonged. Certainly, if Joe didn't become a clown, he would be missing his vocation. On this they were all agreed.

Ever since anyone could remember, Joe had been a bit of a "case," always good for a laugh even when being punished, which was quite often, particularly during this last year. Teachers who had the misfortune to suffer his clowning all looked forward to the day, only a few months hence, when he would have departed for the great world of work. "I pity his employers," one teacher said. "I pity anyone who has to work with him," added another teacher who had just had Joe for an art period.

Actually, whatever the truth of the former teacher's prediction, the latter assessment was probably less than fair. Joe had never had many real friends, but about two years ago he had started going around with two other boys, Arthur Baker and Jack Thomas, all of them in IIC at the time. Neither Baker nor Thomas were exactly model pupils, but for the most part they managed to keep more or less on the right side of the school prefects and hover around the middle of the IIC form list. Joe, on the other hand, who was invariably near the bottom of the form, had already developed a bad name with prefects and masters, who sometimes found his guying of them behind their backs a little hard to take. Whether Baker and Thomas found Joe, or whether he found them, it would be difficult to say, but their alliance seemed only to add to his talents, and woe betide any new master who came the trio's way during the next two years. It was Joe, of course, who could always raise the laugh, whether in adversity or triumph, either by saying or doing the entirely ridiculous whenever it was appropriate or inappropriate, depending on whether you were a member of his audience or the butt of his humour.

Of all the moments most dreaded in the school year, the day when the form lists were read out for the following year

29

was probably the worst. For those boys who went from a low stream to a higher one, and there were not many of these, it was presumably a day of congratulation, but for those who went down there was the disgrace of failure. As failure was one of the worse school crimes, one may assume that the disgrace was real and probably meant to be so. For the vast majority who stayed within their allotted places in the streams it was an occasion, therefore, to be approached with some solemnity and not a little nervousness, and it was a relief when it was finally confirmed that one's place for the following year was unchanged.

Joe managed to remain in the C stream until the fourth year. He had hovered on the brink of going down for two years and had been threatened with demotion on several occasions. Whether by good luck or good management he had been able to avoid the worst, and those who had come up through the school with him had rather taken for granted that he would finish his time as a C boy and leave when he was sixteen. Joe had probably taken this for granted himself, and it came as a surprise when form lists were read out at the end of his third year, and he listened in vain for his name to be included in the list for 4C. At first, he wondered perhaps whether the Senior Master had somehow forgotten to read his name, or whether perhaps he hadn't heard properly, and he had to wait all the way through the reading of the next year's list of 4D before it was confirmed that he had indeed been demoted.

His two friends, who had managed to remain in the C stream, commiserated with him all the way through the next lesson and throughout the break, so that by the end of the morning his good humour seemed to have reasserted itself and he was declaring that as far as 4D was concerned he "was going to have a ball." Term ended two days later, and Joe went off almost immediately on a long holiday with his parents and elder sister.

The following term found Joe in his new form. Joe's reputation had gone before him, and most of the form were therefore a little surprised when he began his first day rather subdued. The clown, it seemed, had lost his touch. Possibly, at this stage, Joe was not too sure of his audience and perhaps not too sure of himself. At break, he went off to look for his two friends, Baker and Thomas. They greeted him briefly, and he listened rather enviously to a description of their escapades during the R.I. lesson. It seemed, however, a little remote as the master who had been taking the lesson was a new one and Joey couldn't even think who he was. Forms sat separately for lunch, so that he was cut off from his friends until the end of the meal.

Lunch, in fact, for Joe was really not very successful. He found himself sitting between two boys who obviously resented his being there and talked across him as though he hardly existed. When the master on duty was not looking or the attention of the prefect in charge of the table otherwise engaged, Joe would find himself physically sandwiched by them. This conduct eventually earned Joe an order mark from the prefect, and he finished the meal feeling alone and miserable. In the yard afterwards Blake and Thomas sympathized with the fact that he had been dumped with "that lot," but the rest of their conversation was about events later that afternoon in which he would have no part. Later he watched an impromptu football match between the rest of the lads in 4C, but the ball never came his way except once, when he caught the ball and it went "over the line." He tossed it to Paterson, a large boy playing half-back. "Good old Joey" said Paterson, and Joe felt life was a little rosier.

By the second day, the newness of the school year had begun to wear off. Joe looked around in 4D for someone whom he might know, but they all looked rather strange still. Lining up outside form rooms he found himself being elbowed out by other boys, and masters who knew him of old were quick to yell at him if he was not in his place when they arrived. Fortunately his old sense of humour was still there and one of his better efforts at mimicry of the Maths. master brought some loud guffaws from his new form mates. He once again sought his old friends during the break, but although their greeting seemed as friendly as ever, Joe felt even more out of things than before. For one thing, a new member had obviously been initiated into the trio—a boy whom Joe had never liked very much. The new boy apparently viewed Joe as an interloper and more or less ignored him. The conversation, in any case, was about things of which Joe knew nothing.

For the rest of the day, Joe was very subdued and even allowed himself to be pushed out of line without more than a murmur. That evening he ate his tea quietly and then disappeared to his room. He reappeared to watch "Softly, softly" on T.V. and spent the rest of the night "glued" to the set. When he went into the kitchen at the end of the evening his father noted that his eyes were red and puffy. "Too much watching that set," he decided.

"Don't you want your glass of milk?" asked his mother. Joe drank it in silence and went to bed.

The next day, he was absolutely on form at school and by the time he went home he had earned two detentions and the wrath of at least three masters. He had seen his old friends from a distance, but they were with the other boy now, and apart from a "Hiya, Joey" from them, they had not spoken to him. He had so far made no new friends in 4D, although most of the boys were now willing to admit that he was "a real case." At home he watched "telly" again all evening. His mother grumbled at the amount of time he spent doing nothing and spoke to him very sharply when she discovered that he'd eaten through a whole packet of biscuits which she'd bought only that afternoon.

"That lad," said his father, "will come to no good." And he added as an afterthought, "No real backbone, that's the trouble with today's generation."

The form mark list at the end of that week showed that Joe was successfully bottom of the form. As a "real case," however, he was now quite established.

Questions for Discussion

1 Why do some people "clown around"?

2 What do you think Joe's real future is likely to be?

3 What would you say was Joe's relationship to his two friends, Baker and Thomas?

4 Supposing you were, for some reason, cut off from your own friends, what might be some of your reactions?

5 Why do you think that Joe became bottom of 4D in that first week? How do you think he felt about himself?

6 Imagine that a newcomer, such as Joe, arrives in your form at the beginning of term. Would you make any effort to welcome him? If so, how would you do it?

7 Role-play one of the incidents on that first day at school, either one of the actual incidents mentioned or one which can be inferred from the case-study. Then discuss either what you observed of the behaviour of the role-players, or how you felt as you took part in the role-play.

8 Imagine that you are a teacher or a prefect who has suffered very badly as a result of Joe's "clowning." Does a teacher in this situation have an obligation to go on being patient and understanding about him? What is the obligation of a prefect?

9 From what little we know about someone like Joe, do you think that there was one time more than any other when he might have been helped by a sympathetic and understanding person? Do you think that anything could be done for him now?

Vicky joins the Gang

At twelve Vicky Warner had been Form-Leader three times, had taken the lead in the Junior Play, and was one of the most popular girls in the Lower School, when her parents told her that she would have to leave because they were moving two hundred miles away.

Vicky felt heart-broken at her parents' decision. She and Pat, her inseparable, special friend, wept together and vowed eternal loyalty, and the Warners promised that Pat should come and stay with them when they got settled in their new home.

The last day of term, Vicky bade a sad good-bye to all her friends in the old school, and the next day she left for the new home her parents had taken in the North.

After a very happy summer, with an exciting holiday abroad, and many letters passing to and fro between Vicky and Pat, Vicky felt much more ready to tackle the thought of her new school. It was an all-age girls' Grammar School, like her previous one, though a little larger, and Vicky was already aware that the girls were much more clothes-conscious in the large northern town where she now lived than they had been in the smaller country town she had left.

The first week of term, however, was a miserable experience for Vicky. The older girls maintained a strict hierarchy and kept the younger girls firmly in their place. No-one seemed ready to offer any help or advice to a new girl. Furthermore, Vicky found that she was the youngest in her new form. Still only twelve, with her thirteenth birthday three months away, she was mixed up with girls who were already fourteen, and the majority were well over thirteen. The whole conversation seemed to centre on boys, clothes, and money. None of these items had even crossed the horizon of Vicky and Pat's conversation at the old school.

The first half of term seemed to last a year, and Vicky cried silently into her pillow many nights, wondering how she could ever establish a point of contact with any of the tightly-knit groups of girls in the form. She recognized that she liked friends and liked to be popular, and she was determined not to give in but to win acceptance somehow.

The group which she picked on as the most likely to accept her, were in fact the group who, as she later found out, were least acceptable to the rest of the school, and to the teachers themselves. Four or five girls, whose general behaviour was considered poor by the staff, they attempted to defy the disapproval they met from classmates and teachers by flaunting their sophisticated clothes and behaviour. The average age of the group was nearly fourteen, their boy-friends were drawn from much older boys, and their academic achievements were far from high.

Vicky made every effort to prove herself acceptable to this group. She quickly adopted ways of behaving and talking which had been utterly strange to her until a few weeks previously. She tried to turn herself overnight from a country-town twelve-year-old into a citified fourteen-year-old. She basked in the warmth of even the partial acceptance she was given by this group, and felt she would die of happiness if they would only let her be really a member of the group.

One day Joan, the leader of the group, asked Vicky solemnly, "Do you really want to join our gang?" Vicky assured her that she wanted that more than anything else.

"Very well," said Joan, "We'll put you on a week's probation. During that time you can be in on everything except the most secret conferences, and at the end of one week we'll let you know our group decision."

The week seemed endless to Vicky, who tried hard not to do or say a thing wrong, and at the same time to persuade the group that she would be a useful member. She told them about her brother, two years older than she was, and

35

promised that he would be able to supply older boys for their parties. At last, in the middle of a geography lesson, when the teacher turned off the lights for a film, Vicky was passed a note from Joan. "You are hereby accepted as a member of our group," it said. Vicky was so relieved she could have cried.

For the rest of that term and the next, Vicky tried hard to re-make herself into a person acceptable to her new gang of friends. She began skipping on her homework for the first time in her life, and received the first bad school report she had ever had. She went to two of the Saturday-night parties, although here she suffered great embarrassment, because her parents insisted on collecting her at ten o'clock, when the parties went on until midnight. At one such party she met a boy of seventeen, who asked her to meet him the next day to go to the pictures. The other girls were very impressed, and she felt that she had really gone up in their eyes by getting a date with a boy so much older.

On the way home after the party, she told her parents about the boy asking for a date, and her father chuckled. She realized later that her parents had not expected her to take the date seriously. In truth, she was a little worried about meeting this boy. All she knew was that his name was "Bandy," and he had told her that he worked in a factory and was on probation for something he hadn't really done. Vicky had a strong feeling that he wasn't exactly the sort of person she knew how to deal with, or the sort of person her parents would understand.

On the other hand, "Bandy" was nice, and he had been kind to her, and he was the first boy-friend she had ever had, so she was quite determined to go to meet him in town the next afternoon. When her mother realized what was happening, she forbade Vicky to go. Vicky saw that her mother was trying to be reasonable, and to explain why she couldn't go out with a boy she didn't really know, when she was only just thirteen. Her mother didn't realize that she just couldn't disappoint him by not turning up. What would she tell the others on Monday?

Mrs. Warner finally agreed to go to meet "Bandy" herself, and explain that it wasn't Vicky's fault that she hadn't come. Knowing her mother was trying to be kind, but feeling utterly out of her depth and lost, Vicky flung herself down on her bed and burst into tears. When her mother sat down beside her she put her head on her mother's shoulder, saying, "Why can't I go back to my old school? I miss Pat so terribly much, and all my own friends. I keep thinking I'll see them coming round the next corner in the corridor any minute, and then they don't. I don't really like Joan and her group in the same way. They're all right but they just aren't like my old friends. Mummy, I'm so homesick, I don't know who I am any more."

Questions for Discussion

1 Was Vicky too easily upset by the strangeness of a new school? Where could she have turned for help?

2 Do you think if Vicky had waited, she might have found friends nearer her own age and interests?

3 What do you think of groups who put new members "on probation"? Is this a kind way to behave?

4 Would you have insisted on going to meet "Bandy" if you had been Vicky?

5 What do you think would have happened if Vicky's parents had let her go to meet "Bandy"?

6 What do you think Vicky should do now? Are her friends more important than her school-work?

One Boy

At fifteen, George Palmer, known familiarly in his form as Georgieboy, was a rather lanky ungainly lad with the first signs of a fair stubble of beard which threatened to extend his untidy sideboards. His teachers in Highcliffe Comprehensive School saw him as a rather characterless boy with a tendency to day-dreaming—bright enough, though, without any doubt.

The oldest of three children in his family, at school he kept himself to himself, and after four years, even the older boys usually left him alone. He seemed to show little interest in girls, and at the school's social gatherings he wandered about with very little apparent enthusiasm for what was going on.

George had come to the Highcliffe Comprehensive from a small church primary school, where his career had been comparatively uneventful. Although he had been a slow beginning reader, once he had mastered the mechanics of reading he had become an avid member of the school library, and if ever he got into trouble it was invariably because he was caught with a book under his desk when he should have been doing something else. He never caused any serious trouble and his teachers thought unanimously that with his I.Q. of 117 George was certainly a bright hope for the school. Whatever else he was, he was also clean. His nails were always cut, and unlike the majority of his classmates he invariably smelled of soap and water.

George's mother had been a nurse before her marriage to George's father, who was a skilled pattern-maker in a tool and jig manufacturer's. She had been for an interview with George's primary school Head in his last year at primary school. When George's mother had suggested that she would like her son to sit the examinations for the old direct grant grammar school, the Head had advised that her son would probably be better off at Highcliffe. "At the grammar school, George would probably not get into the top stream—his maths. are still slower than they should be—so that his chances of 'O' levels would be much smaller. At Highcliffe, with its wide range of subjects, and where transfer from stream to stream is always possible, a late developer like George would have many more opportunities. I'm sure George has something, and I would like to see him achieve success for himself." George had, accordingly, gone on to Highcliffe, where, in a twelve form entry, he had found himself in the D form.

He knew very few boys and girls in his form. The majority had come from other schools—very few from George's own primary school, most of whom were in the lower streams of the school.

There was the occasional fracas between boys in the top streams and those at the very bottom, where some of the real toughs of the neighbourhood had congregated. But usually they could be made to work out their hostilities on the football field, and the houses system certainly helped to make this possible.

To George Palmer, at the age of eleven, his first term had seemed rather bewildering. It was all right when he was in class, but outside the hundreds of children with whom he came in contact seemed a huge crowd from which he needed to be insulated. The quieter boys seemed to be in the streams above him. At register time he sat by Jameson, a boy from the A Form, who, he had discovered, came from another part of the town. Once or twice he had been to visit him in the small detached house where he lived, in one of the quieter suburbs. Jameson's parents were both teachers, and Jameson's father, who taught rural science at a school elsewhere in the County, kept his garden immaculate. George sometimes dreamed that when he was grown up he would have a house and garden like the Jameson's.

George worked hard that first year and came out sixth overall in his form. One girl moved up to 2C as a result of the end of year exams. When he came back to school for the second year, he thought that now, as there wasn't so much

39

competition, he might do well enough to get out of the D stream into the stream above. He was determined to work very hard, for he hated the workshop periods, which were compulsory for all the D stream boys, and longed to have the chance of choosing physics and chemistry instead. At Christmas he came out fourth. "You would do even better if you could work a bit faster," said his maths. teacher. In social studies, his teachers agreed that he had worked hard, but his P.E. master thought that he needed to try more. English was far and away his best subject.

Because he seemed to have done well that term, his mother and father bought him a brief-case for Christmas. Usually only the boys in the A and B streams carried brief-cases. It marked them out from the rest, who, for their part, called them snobs. The boys from the bottom stream said, "They ain't nothing. They can't fight and they talk so prissy—like a lot of girls. They think we're stupid. But they'll be the stupid ones when we're earning twenty pounds a week in the dirty room at the factory and they're still in this place."

When George arrived at school with his new case he got a bit of teasing from some of his class mates, but he was quite unprepared for the attack last thing on Friday of the first week of term. He'd gone into the cloak room to collect his coat and cap, and there were a group of boys from his old primary school there. One of them shouted out "Here's Georgieboy with his brief-case. Where'd you get it, Georgie? Did your momma buy it, Georgie? No, his old man nicked it. Good old Georgie." Then one of them ran at him, knocking him against the cloakroom pegs, grabbing the brief-case and tossing it across to the group. "Hey!" said George, and he moved towards the group to get his case back. The next thing he knew, he was on the ground, with two of the boys holding him. The rest were laughing, tossing his case from one to another. "Hey!" he shouted, "That's my case. Let it alone." But they only shouted louder, and one of the boys holding him twisted his arm. When they heard a prefect coming, they left him. His coat was torn, and he felt blood from the back of his head where it had hit the concrete floor. His brief-case was scratched, the handle pulled off, and all his books scattered and crumpled on the floor. Next day, even the A stream boys made fun of him, in their superior way. "What's happened to your brief-case, Georgieboy?" "That'll teach you not to get ideas above your station." He never took his brief-case back to school, but left it stuffed at the bottom of his cupboard at home.

He came out third in his form at the end of that year. "He should try harder to mix socially," wrote his housemaster. In the third year he had met Jameson in the local coffee bar. Jameson had another boy with him, from the A form. "Aren't you one of the workshop lot?" said Jameson's friend. Afterwards he had ignored George pointedly. Jameson was never very friendly to George after that, and seemed embarrassed when they met.

One boy was promoted at the end of the third year, but not George. He maintained his place about third from the top. His English was still good, and he enjoyed maths., but his craft and mechanical drawing dragged down his average. Most teachers, except his English teacher, thought he wasn't going to make much of himself and described him as "a bit of a mouse." Then, in the first term of his fourth year, George produced the best average of his school career, and came out first in his class. His form tutor called him in. "I have put you down as a G.C.E. candidate," he said, "I believe that you have it in you to get enough 'O' levels next year to go the Sixth. I think you should try." George seemed quieter than ever during that second term, and when the Easter results came out, he had dropped to eighth in class. "You can do better than this, Palmer," said his tutor. "Frankly, any lad who writes English as you do, ought to have been out of this stream long ago. Is there anything we can do to help you?" George did not answer. "Is it your speed in maths. that's bringing you down? You'll just have to get down to it this term."

At the end of the year, George was fifteenth in class. His tutor called him. "What's the matter with you, Palmer?" George looked across the desk at him. "I don't want to go on with school, sir. I'm finishing this term and not coming back."

Questions for Discussion

1 Was George's Primary School Headmaster right, in thinking that he would do better at the big Comprehensive school than at the small Grammar School?

2 How do you think the other pupils at Highcliffe saw George?

3 Do you think Jameson is a snob?

4 Why did the other boys attack George after he brought his new brief-case to school?

5 Why did George start to do badly during his fourth year at school?

6 What should George do, when he leaves school, to make sure he is happier at work than he was at school?

7 Was there anything George could have done to make himself a bit happier when he was in the first two years of secondary school?

8 Did George make the right decision, when he chose to leave school at fifteen?

Romance in Paris

Wendy went to Paris with her older sister, Freda, when she was almost seventeen. She had hopes of returning to school to take "A" levels, and get a place at university. She was a very lively girl, with dark curly hair, blue eyes, and a cheeky smile. Wendy liked boys, and had lots of boy friends at her school, but she had avoided anything too serious in the way of boy-involvements, as she really did badly want to have that place at university.

Wendy's older sister was a much more serious-minded person than Wendy, and was training as a psychiatric nurse. Both girls had done equally well at school, and they enjoyed each other's company well enough, though Wendy did sometimes feel a great temptation to shock her sister by outrageous behaviour.

It may have been one such occasion that began the whole story of Wendy's future, and changed the course of her life. The two girls had gone into a pavement café for their lunch-time sandwich, when a group of three young Australians came into the café, and sat next to them. There was a handsome man, whom Wendy took to be about twenty-one, and a couple who held hands and exchanged private jokes, rather ignoring their companion.

As the time came for Wendy to leave with her sister, she deliberately winked at the young Australian, and said, "Poor fellow, why is such a handsome chap all on his own then?" Before her elder sister could intervene, the man had grabbed Wendy on to his knee, and said, "There now, I'm not alone any more, am I?" Wendy was enjoying herself, and persuaded Freda to stay with the Australians, and share their table and chatter for another hour.

By the time Wendy could be made to tear herself away, they had learned that the young man, Ben, was a poet, living in a cottage he had rented just on the outskirts of Paris. They had arranged to meet again that evening, and Freda was well aware that she was only included in the invitation for courtesy. Ben had hardly taken his eyes from Wendy's face the whole hour.

The last eight days of the sisters' Paris trip became entirely taken over by Ben, sometimes with his two friends and

43

Freda included in the outings, but more often, Ben and Wendy disappeared on their own for hours at a time. When the time came for them to leave, Wendy told her sister that Ben had asked her to go and live with him in his cottage. "It's a gorgeous little cottage, Freda," she said, "And I really do love Ben, you know."

"You're not serious, Wendy," said Freda, appalled. "You can't get married yet. What about your 'A' levels, and your career? And anyway, Ben's years older than you."

"Of course I'm not going to marry him—anyway, his divorce from his first wife hasn't come through, so I couldn't marry him anyway. Actually, he's twenty-eight, but don't tell the parents that, or that he's married, will you? Promise?"

Hoping that this was the last they would hear of Ben, and only too ready to agree to keep her parents from finding how inadequate her supervision had been, Freda promised to let Wendy tell only the edited version of her romance. When they arrived home, however, she was to find that this was by no means the last of Ben. Daily letters arrived, flowers, phone calls, all vowing that he could not live without Wendy. Wendy obviously found herself very touched, and not a little flattered by this, and began to walk around with a pensive and dramatically tragic air.

Freda had to return to her teaching hospital before the results of her sister's "O" levels arrived, and so was not able to offer any cheer, when Wendy discovered that in English, her favourite subject, and the one she intended to read at University, she had only got a poor grade of 5, although in other subjects she had not done badly at all. After three days attempting to absorb the shock, Wendy announced to her parents that she was not going on to the VIth form, and that she was going back to Paris to live with Ben.

Wendy and Freda's parents were enlightened and "modern" parents. Her father was a lecturer in art, and her mother was a teacher, and both had always vowed that their children's happiness was more important to them than any rules of morality. They questioned Wendy closely, as to whether she was really in love with Ben, and she assured them that she was. They felt that Ben had certainly proved his feelings by the letters and gifts he had sent, and they were reassured that they would retain their daughter's affection, and their own image of themselves as modern parents, if they let her go.

Ben was waiting to meet Wendy at the airport when she arrived in Paris, and when she told him that yesterday had been her seventeenth birthday, he took her out for a wonderful celebration in the most expensive restaurant she had ever seen. For weeks Wendy was deliriously happy. She came to worship Ben, and was able to forgive him the terrible rages he would suffer from time to time. He drank an enormous amount at this time, as much as a bottle of whisky in a day, and then afterwards he would beg her forgiveness, and cry like a child.

Despite her comparative youth, Wendy often felt more of a mother to Ben. He was terrified if she disappeared for ten minutes, and he was frantically possessive. He always slept with a revolver in the bedside table, and couldn't sleep in the dark. The more she stayed with him, the more Wendy loved him. By her eighteenth birthday, she had grown up, she sometimes felt, more than her mother had done at forty. Ben's divorce had come through—she found the papers from his Australian solicitor accidentally one day—but he made no mention of marrying her, and amongst the group of Australian and American expatriate young people in which they moved, this did not seem very important.

Wendy had been with Ben for two years when she realized that he was staying out at night with another woman—an American in her early thirties. With a wisdom beyond her years, Wendy decided to say nothing, in the hope that Ben might tire of the older woman, and she wouldn't lose him.

One night, though, Ben came home, very drunk, with the older woman beside him. He looked at Wendy as if she was a stranger. "Get out!" was all he said—and repeated it when she seemed slow to understand.

At eleven-thirty at night, with only a few francs in her pocket—the equivalent of about twelve shillings—Wendy found herself alone in the streets of Paris. She had not had time to pack her clothes, all she had was a book of Ben's poems, and her own typewriter, on which she had intended once to write great literature.

Two days later, thanks to a loan from the Australian couple who had been her friends as well as Ben's, she arrived back at her parents' home in England.

Questions for Discussion

1 What can we know about the relationship between Wendy and her sister Freda?

2 Was Wendy's behaviour in the café bad manners, silly, or quite normal for when you are on holiday abroad?

3 Can you name several factors which made Wendy decide to go and live with Ben?

4 Was Wendy in love with Ben? Why do you think so?

5 What were Ben's feelings towards Wendy throughout the incident?

6 Were Wendy's parents right to let her go to Paris to live with Ben? What might have happened if they had said "No"?

7 Could Wendy have acted any differently at the break-up of her relationship with Ben?

The Apprentice's First Date

Jim Hodson left the Dale County Secondary School for Boys with a fair record of achievement behind him although he was no great scholar. He was in the top five of the B Form, had played for the school football team, and had managed to keep himself out of any serious trouble. "A good, hard-working lad who would do well," prophesied his Head-master.

On the day he left, Jim became apprenticed to a local plumber, and every week from thence on Jim brought home his weekly pay packet and, like his father before him, proudly placed it on the table for his mother. In fact, Mrs. Hodson took only the bare minimum for Jim's board and keep. The rest of his pay she handed back to him as an allowance from which he was supposed to clothe himself, and pay for his own entertainment. Some of this, Jim put away towards the day when he would be able to take out his first licence to ride a motorcycle.

Jim had been out with one or two girls, although about none of them had he felt at all seriously. Much of his time he spent with his own gang of friends, all of whom he had known at school. Some nights they would go to the Youth Club, a business-like red-brick building with its own coffee-bar, discotheque, and well-equipped games room. Usually, at the weekly Saturday night dance, Jim would stand on the edge of the dance floor, wolf-whistling the girls, drinking coke and really not doing very much else. To Jim it was all very warm and friendly. He felt a part of his crowd and was happy with his life as it was going.

One Saturday night, all this changed. It began as a half-hearted dare. Jim had been standing with the usual stag group on the edge of the dance floor when a couple of rather pretty girls, both strangers to the club, had taken to the floor. Jim's gang whistled. "Betcher couldn't break that two up," said one of the group to Jim. "Betcher," said Jim, and it was at the end of two dances later that Jim found himself drinking coke with the more attractive of the two.

Jean, Jim's newly-found girl friend, said she was fifteen.

47

She was still at school, she said. She thought the Club was O.K. The discotheque was really "super." She left just before ten, having had a "super time." By this time Jim decided that she was quite the prettiest girl he'd ever seen, and he wondered whether he would meet her again.

The week went by. Friday evening came. Jim wondered whether Jean would be at the Club on Saturday night. "Why don't you phone her?" said his gang. "Don't be daft," said Jim. "Catch me calling up any bird." "We'll all phone her," they chanted, as they stood beside the red telephone kiosk outside the butcher's. The telephone kiosk and the nearby bus shelter were the local meeting places for the youth of the neighbourhood and on this night, as on other nights of the week, there were an assortment of motor-cycles and scooters propped against the kerb. Occasionally some lad would climb on to his bike, rev. the engine, and roar up and down the street. It was a noisy place, and whenever anyone decided to make a phone call it was always with everyone crowding into the kiosk, the door open, and a background racket of catcalls and motor-cycle engines. "All right," said Jim, "only shut the door, will you." His gang jeered and made faces outside the box, as he dialled the number.

A man's voice answered. It sounded educated and authoritative.

Jim swallowed. "Can I speak to Jean, please?"

"Who's that calling?" said the man.

"It's Jim Hodson," and Jim felt as though he was back at school. He could feel himself blushing, and he shook his fist at the grinning faces outside.

A minute later he heard Jean's voice. It sounded distant, and he felt his heart miss a beat. "Yes?" she said.

"This is Jim . . . , you know, the boy at the Club last week."

"Oh, yes," said Jean.

48

"I just wanted to know whether you were coming to the Club tomorrow night, that's all."

"Well, maybe. I'd have to ask my parents about their arrangements. I think we're going out to dinner. I'd love to otherwise."

"Oh," said Jim. "I see." He felt less than life-size.

Jean didn't appear that Saturday, nor the next. Then they met, quite accidentally, in the local record shop. She had the same girl with her as had been with her at the dance on the first occasion.

"Hello," she said. "Buying records?" She hardly waited for a reply. "This is my friend Sylvie. Isn't Number One just super this week?" Jim nodded. He couldn't think of anything really smart to say. Jean chattered on. She and Sylvie were just off to do the shops and then they were having tea out at Brockton's. Jim had seen Brockton's but it was not the sort of place he would have visited. He felt more comfortable in the local coffee-bar.

"Going to the Club dance on Saturday, are you?" he finally asked.

"Thought of," said Jean. "If Sylvie will come."

Jim plunged. "Look, if I brought a friend along, we could go together, couldn't we?" He glanced at Sylvie. "He's a really good friend of mine."

"Well . . . ," Jean hesitated.

"Yes, let's. Do let's," said Sylvie. "It would be super."

And so it was arranged. There was, however, no question of meeting at the Club. Jean was quite adamant that Jim and his friend would have to come to her house and call for them. Jim had some little trouble in getting his friend Bill to agree to this arrangement, but nevertheless, duly at eight o'clock the next Saturday, the two boys presented themselves at the front door of Jean's home, a detached house in one of the town's new developments. A late model car stood in the driveway. The door was opened by Jean's mother.

"It's Jim, isn't it? Do come in. Jean and Sylvia won't be very long," and she ushered them into the sitting room. "Perhaps you wouldn't mind waiting in here." As Bill said afterwards, "It just stank of class."

Jean's father was a short, well-dressed man. He shook hands with the two boys and asked whether they'd been to the match that afternoon. They chatted for a few minutes until the two girls appeared. To Jim he seemed a pleasant enough man.

"Don't keep her out late," said Jean's father. "And have a good time."

At the Club, Jim bought Jean a coke. "You shouldn't," she said. "I have my own money."

They danced once, but Jim was very aware of his own shortcomings as a dancer. Jean was a beautiful dancer—very, very cool. Then they joined Sylvie and Bill again. Bill seemed to be getting on all right. He had a brand of quick repartee which Jim envied but which he knew he could never equal in a thousand years. Jean was chattering away, and she seemed hardly to notice his own verbal inadequacies. He felt he couldn't ask her for another dance yet. He was a rotten dancer anyway.

They stood on the edge of the floor. Bill and Sylvie were already out there, Bill looking as though he really belonged.

Then Donovan came in, with a group of other boys. Donovan lived only a few doors away from Jim. He was a year older and in the VIth Form of the local grammar school. Donovan was known to be very smooth, and he already ran around in an old M.G. It was quite unusual that he should appear in the local club. Anyhow, here he was, looking smoother than ever.

Jean saw him almost as soon as Jim, and when she smiled at him Donovan came over. The next thing Jim realized, Jean was on the dance floor with Donovan. Jim felt bitter and very lost and empty. He waited through four more dances, then he saw his gang coming across to him.

"Lost your bird, Jim?" they called at him.

"No," said Jim, and he thought to himself "and I really never had her." "Who's for a pint? This kid's place really gets me. Let's find a man's place."

He looked across at Jean, still with Donovan. He felt lost again. Then the warmth of the gang flooded over him as they elbowed and pushed together through the door. What was a bird, anyhow? Just another bird.

Questions for Discussion

1 How do you think Jim really felt about Jean?

2 What do you think Jean felt about Jim?

3 What do you think of Jean's behaviour at the dance? If you had been in Jim's place, what would you have done?

4 How do you think Jim would feel towards girls after the incident of the dance?

5 If you had been in Jean's place, how would you have felt when you had discovered that Jim had left you with Donovan at the dance?

6 If you had been in Jim's place, would you have asked Jean to go out with you in the beginning? If you had been Jean, would you have accepted his invitation?

Maureen

Maureen was fifteen, and she was in love for the first time. Not a particularly pretty girl, she had become used to being ignored or laughed at by boys ever since the difference between boys and girls had become an "interesting" fact of life. Earlier, until about the age of nine, she had got on very well with boys, and in fact had played with two boys

51

across the street more than with other girls. Then had come the great divide between the sexes. Before she could herself understand what was happening, boys became something to giggle over, or to pursue by means of ostentatious retreat, and above all to brood over and discuss as the most important thing in life.

Although not unaware of the feelings which lay behind this behaviour, Maureen had found herself obliged to play the part of confidante and observer of her friends' relationships with boys, since she found that most boys were not interested in her. Indeed, she had ceased to try and interest them from the very first mixed party she had ever attended, when only twelve. At this party the boys and the girls were all given cards with pictures drawn on them, indicating half a flower or fruit, and the first game was to find who had been given the other "half" of the picture on your card. This person, who would be of the opposite sex, would then be your "partner" for the entire evening. Great excitement had reigned during the period when everyone had searched for the correct partner and often the boys had made gallant remarks as they found the girl whose card matched theirs. Maureen's partner, however, had taken one look at her and said "Oh no!" He had then refused to speak to her for the rest of the evening.

That was the last time Maureen tried to get along with boys until just after her fourteenth birthday. That summer, she had gone to Wales with her parents, and in the field opposite their bungalow, a boys' school was holding its summer camp. After several hopeful glances across the hedge, three of the boys finally worked up their courage to come and invite Maureen and two other girls who were holidaying next door, to their "camp-fire."

It was there she had met sixteen-year-old John, and the most incredible and wonderful thing happened; he fell for her. They played tennis together, went swimming together, and of course went walking in the sand dunes where he kissed her passionately.

To their delight, they found that their homes were only a few miles apart, so that they were able to meet regularly throughout the winter. Although they did go out to the cinema, and occasionally to a coffee-bar, most often they met only to find a place in a field on the outskirts of town where they could make more and more passionate love. Each meeting the petting "went a little further," and John would plead insistently to let him "go all the way."

Maureen felt herself torn agonizingly into two halves. One half loved John, was aroused and moved by his passionate love-making, wanted to please him and was afraid of losing him. The other half suffered searing guilt, partly towards her deeply religious parents, but even more towards a God whom she felt she had already offended by the intimacies she had allowed. She went to church on Sunday mornings, and prayed desperately for strength to be a "good woman." She met John on Sunday afternoons and was carried away all over again by the excitement of love-making, and pride in having a boy so completely captivated by her.

At Christmas, Maureen's parents agreed to let Maureen and her seventeen-year-old sister spend a week in London on their own. Maureen agreed with John that they should meet in London, away from her parents' constant vigilance, and promised to write to him, arranging a time and place where they could meet. This she did as soon as she arrived in London, and posted the letter in the hotel's private letter box. She received no answer until many weeks later, when John wrote and said "You didn't bother to let me know when I could come to London, so I don't care about you any more. I've found another girl now," However, he ended the letter, "Yours as ever," and put "kisses" at the bottom.

Maureen wrote back immediately, explaining that she had written to him, and had wanted him to meet her in

London. The very next day, John arrived to meet her after school. She was delighted to see him, but embarrassed that he should see her in school uniform and frustrated that they could not go anywhere private to make up the quarrel properly. John told her that he had arranged to meet his new girl friend on Sunday, and said that he could not now cancel the arrangement. He arranged to meet Maureen beforehand for half-an-hour.

On Sunday afternoon, Maureen dressed very carefully, put on some eye make-up for the first time, and went to meet John. He seemed as much in love with her as ever, and Maureen tried to indicate that soon she would be prepared to "go all the way." John left her reluctantly, promising to get rid of the other girl, Patricia, and to phone her later on.

Maureen went home and waited for the phone to ring. At nine o'clock that night it rang at last, and John's voice said, all in one breathless sentence, "I promised to ring you up and let you know—well, I'm sorry but I've thought about it and it's 'Tricia that I love. Good-bye."

Maureen went up to her room, undressed, and went to bed. She lay all night watching the pattern of the moonlight upon the ceiling as it moved across the room. It was the longest night of her life. She didn't even cry.

Questions for Discussion

1 In what ways do you think Maureen's experience of boys before she met John, affected her behaviour with him?

2 How do you think Maureen felt when her "partner" would not speak to her at the party?

3 Why do you think Maureen went on meeting John when the relationship made her feel guilty and unhappy?

4 Do you think that Maureen was a truly religious person?

5 Do you think it would have helped Maureen to talk to her parents?

54

6 What kind of a boy do you think John was?

7 Do you think that John really received the letter Maureen had written from London?

8 Why do you think John broke off the relationship so soon after having tried to take it up again?

9 What do you think are John's real feelings about Maureen?

10 What do you think are Maureen's real feelings about John?

Two Girls and Two Brothers

Barbara and Jenny were very close friends, although Jenny was eight months older than Barbara. The two girls lived close together, had been to school together all their lives, and were in the same form, despite the gap in their ages.

The two girls were different, however, in many important ways. Jenny's father had died when Jenny was only seven, and her mother had been forced to work late hours as long as Jenny could remember. This meant that Jenny had a great deal of freedom and was often able to entertain her friends in her home in the evenings while her mother was out. In fact, Jenny and her mother did not really ever seem very close, and Jenny often complained that her mother was "nosey" and "sneaky," opening her letters, and trying to read her diary.

Barbara's parents, in contrast, were extremely strict, and insisted on Barbara being in by nine at the latest, even when she was fourteen and a half. The only connection between Barbara's mother and Jenny's mother, Barbara often said, was that they were both highly suspicious-natured, at least where their daughters were concerned.

Actually, although Jenny, like Barbara, had never given

her mother the slightest reason for her suspicions before her fifteenth birthday, Barbara privately thought that Jenny really had become boy-crazy in the last two or three months, and the sort of boy Jenny was mixed up with worried her friend considerably.

The most recent boy in Jenny's life was a boy of eighteen called Dave. Certainly, life with Dave seemed to involve Jenny in a lot of excitement, which Barbara rather envied, but she herself did not like Dave at all. He was far too sophisticated and smooth, and so very much older than any other boys that she and Jenny had ever met. Dave had a younger brother, Brian, who asked Barbara if she would go out with him. He seemed a nice enough boy and, at sixteen, he still seemed very grown-up to Barbara, so she agreed to go out with him once or twice, even though she disliked his brother.

The four young friends began to go out together quite often, and when their money ran out, they would go over to Jenny's house, and spend the evening listening to records, or watching an occasional television show. At least, Barbara and Brian did this, but more and more often, Jenny and her boy-friend would disappear upstairs to the bedroom, and it was obvious that things had gone far beyond what Barbara felt was proper between them. She was truly shocked when Jenny confided in her that she and Dave were having inter-course regularly together. Jenny offered to explain to Barbara how she could buy contraceptives to "make it safe."

Not long after this conversation, Brian began trying to persuade Barbara that they too should, as he said, "Go all the way," like his brother and Jenny. He had had a long talk with Dave, and he assured Barbara that he knew how to make it perfectly safe. What possible objections could there be?

"What ever would people say, if they knew?" countered Barbara. "No-one is going to know," replied Brian.

"Boys expect their wives to be virgins—I would be making myself cheap," Barbara argued again.

"That's old-fashioned now," Brian replied. "Anyway, what happens is between you and me, darling, and I promise you will never seem cheap to me."

"What if I had a baby?" was Barbara's last reservation—and it was harder to think up reasons, now, because Brian was making love to her while he talked, and she couldn't help enjoying it.

"I've told you, silly, I know how to make it all completely safe." Brian reminded her, and she could think of no more arguments at that moment.

Later, however, she regretted what had happened immensely. She had not really enjoyed her first experience of sex, and furthermore, she found that Brian and she had less to say to each other than they had ever had before. Each seemed to find the other embarrassing, and from then on, although they went out occasionally with Dave and Jenny, they never attempted to make love any more.

A month or two later, though, Barbara found herself in for an even more upsetting experience. She went home with Jenny after school, and to their surprise, Jenny's mother was already home. She told them both to sit down, and then she really let fly, as Jenny said afterwards. She had found a letter of Dave's in Jenny's school satchel, in which Dave had referred to their relationship in terms which left no doubt as to just how far things had gone. She was absolutely furious with both girls, accusing Barbara of being no better, and even of encouraging Jenny, by the way she had carried on with Brian. She told Jenny that she forbade her ever to see Dave again, and threatened to tell Barbara's parents all about her and Brian, if the two of them had anything to do with either brother again.

Jenny was terribly depressed for weeks after this, and would pour out her troubles to Barbara at school. She and her

57

mother were having endless rows and fights, and Jenny felt she could bear it no longer.

Matters had obviously come to a head one Friday night, although the first that Barbara knew about it was when a policewoman came to her home, and asked to speak to her. She told her that Jenny had run away from home, and asked Barbara if she could tell them where Jenny might have gone. Barbara quite truthfully said she knew nothing about it, but the policewoman asked her mother to let them know immediately if they had any information, or if Jenny made any move to get in touch with Barbara. The police had also sent one man over to Dave's house, to interview him and his parents, and Barbara wondered how he and Brian were getting on with their questioning.

Later, Barbara learnt that Jenny had turned up at Dave's house, and been escorted home by the police. Jenny was put on probation, though Barbara never learned why, and she was never allowed to speak to Jenny again. Jenny was sent off to the technical college the following year, and never returned to school.

Two days after Jenny's attempt to run away, though, the same policewoman as before came back to Barbara's house, and interviewed her again. She seemed to know all about Barbara and Brian, though Barbara really wondered what possible business of the police that could be, and she questioned Barbara very closely about the events at Jenny's house on the nights when her mother had been away.

Barbara was relieved that she heard no more from the police, at least, but her life from then on, at home, was a misery. Her mother never let her out one single evening, not even at week-ends. She was never allowed to contact Jenny, or speak to her. If she was as much as ten minutes late home from school, her mother came out searching for her. Sometimes Barbara was tempted to follow Jenny's example, and run away.

Questions for Discussion

1 How much can Barbara blame her troubles on the fact that Jenny was an older girl, and led her on?

2 Why did Jenny become so involved in her relationship with Dave?

3 Were the girls wrong to have intercourse with their boy-friends?

4 Does the age of the couple, or the time they have known each other, make any difference to the rights and wrongs of pre-marital sex?

5 What do you think of Brian's arguments to Barbara?

6 Was Jenny's mother justified in hunting through her daughter's possessions, and reading her letters?

7 What do you think of Jenny's action in running away from home? Was there any other action she could have taken?

8 What rights do the police have in a case such as this, to question the girls' friends?

Pete

Pete had left school when he was sixteen, with three "O" levels to his credit, an interest in mechanical drawing, and a passion for engines of any kind. His elder sister, who had been to university and was now teaching in a girl's high school, had not been surprised when he had failed to gain a grammar school place at eleven, and had predicted that probably all that he would ever do would be "to mess about with things. As long as he was happy, did this really matter?" she would say.

Pete's parents, however, were not reassured by their daughter's advice and had spent more hours than they cared to remember, discussing when their son was going to settle down and do something with his life. But anxious as they both often were, they consoled themselves with the thought that as long as he was happy with what he was doing he was bound to come out all right in the end.

He stayed on at school for an additional year, and his first job on leaving seemed very promising. He became a student apprentice at a large engineering company, and for one day every week he would go along to the local technical college for an O.N.C. course in engineering. When his parents asked him how he was getting on, he invariably replied, "Oh, all right," but among his friends he admitted that he found the apprenticeship a bit boring sometimes. When he was not at technical college he would sit around for hours in a corner of the shop floor, just talking. He cast envious eyes towards the drawing office. He went in there occasionally and felt that if only he could have started here instead of engineering all his interest and skill in mechanical drawing could have been used. He made a few inquiries about transferring to be a draughtsman, but he was told that the firm had no vacancies.

It was about this time that he got his first motor-cycle. He had always been keen on motor-cycle racing. He had seen his first T.T. on the Isle of Man when he was only ten, and still remembered the magic that the noise of the engines and the sight of the riders streaking by the stand had meant for him. From the time he had been allowed to go off alone on his bike for any distance he had followed hill climbs and local meetings, and as soon as he had had enough pocket money he had become an ardent fan of the city's track team.

Pete's first motor-cycle therefore was a great event. He learned to ride it quite quickly and after twelve months he was already competing in local amateur events. He now attended most of the big meetings in the country, and he lived in the hope that someone would either notice him or somehow he would eventually make a national name. There was no doubt that he had the makings of a good rider and with a lot of hard work and some luck he might go far.

He was finding it more and more difficult to concentrate on his job at the engineering company. The O.N.C. course was fairly demanding, and he felt that if he only had more time he could concentrate on developing his motor-cycle riding. At the end of a year as an apprentice, he had managed to save fifty pounds and he made the decision to give up his job and really get down to developing his skill as a rider. His mother and father were a little worried by the turn of events, but they agreed to help him for a maximum of two months. Things, however, went badly for Pete. He had engine troubles from the beginning and weather turned out to be appalling, and after eight weeks he had to admit that he was getting nowhere. His money was now gone, so he decided, as an emergency measure to carry him over for the next few months, to get a job which would leave his day-time free. The first evening job that was offered to him was that of dishwasher at a restaurant on the nearby motorway. The money wasn't too bad, but he found that during the day he felt too tired to do very much. It was obvious that he had to get some sort of job which was more in line with his ambitions as a professional rider.

He tried all the obvious places. The local track had nothing, and he did the round of all the motor-cycle agencies without any result. Although he had already a fair amount of experience with engines, he had no real qualification to offer any garage, and the only job he could find was that of petrol attendant on the forecourt of one of the large motor dealers. Pete found that this was a busy life, and he enjoyed meeting the hundreds of motorists who passed through the forecourt every day. When he got home at night, however, he felt so tired that even tinkering about with his motor-bike seemed too great an effort. It came as no surprise and was some relief to his parents when he said that he was giving up this job too. He wanted to do something with his life and he admitted that a forecourt attendant was no way to the top.

61

He mooned around at home for nearly a month. He went on several interviews arranged for him by the Employment Officer, but nothing came of any of them. He still felt that mechanical drawing was his best subject and that given a chance he would do really well with it. Perhaps he could become a designer, but no one seemed to be able to tell him how to set about becoming one. When his sister was home one week-end, he plucked up his courage to ask if she knew how he could become one. She was quite sympathetic but admitted that she hadn't the faintest idea. In any case she was certain that any top designer was bound to have a university degree. Pete began to feel that it was hopeless. Finally, his uncle helped him to find a job in the office of a small manufacturer.

Pete discovered himself doing everything from daily accounts to interviewing salesmen, and for the first time, in helping to compile a new catalogue, he found his skill at drawing useful. Unfortunately, his salary was now really not much better than when he had started out as a student apprentice, and as far as he could see in his present job he was never likely to do very much better. He still had the pull of his motor-cycle riding, and he was convinced that given the right break he could move into the top professional league. Most week-ends he spent away from home haunting the national meetings, and as a local rider he had developed a fair name for dash and guts over rough country.

He was now nineteen, lanky and probably rather good-looking in a gangling sort of way. No one had ever known him to go out with a girl, and his mother had begun to wonder whether he was the kind of son who would be at home with his parents for the rest of their lives. Then, one evening, he asked whether he could bring a girl home for the week-end. Apparently he had met her at a meeting near Birmingham a short time before. After the initial surprise, his parents agreed.

Mary turned out, in fact, to be a rather attractive girl of eighteen who was training to be a nurse. Pete seemed to be genuinely fond of her, and she of him. When Pete's mother and father were alone together later in the first evening that week-end, they agreed that Mary seemed just the girl for Pete.

"If only he would settle down to something really sensible in life," said his mother. She sighed. "Perhaps he will, now."

Questions for Discussion

1 Do you think that Pete's first job was the right one for him?

2 If you had been a friend of Pete's at any time during the first two years after leaving school, what would your advice to him have been?

3 What was Pete's real problem?

4 What do you think may happen to Pete's career now that he has met Mary?

5 Suppose you were Mary and were genuinely fond of Pete. Assuming that you somehow learned about his past job "pattern," what would you say to him now?

6 Did Pete's family behave correctly with him? Was there anything any of them did wrong? Or were there other things they might have done for him?

7 How can someone like Pete make the very best use of the talents he has? To whom could he turn for advice?

8 You have possibly already decided what your own career is going to be. See whether you can list all the reasons for your own choice. What do you really know about your chosen career? What do you still need to know? How can you find out more?

Marriage or College?

When her "O" level results came in, Susan began to believe at last that her hopes for a university place might just be realistic. She had really done better than she expected, and at sixteen she had high hopes of becoming a prefect and enjoying her Sixth Form years very much.

The two years before "O" levels had really been the most incredibly hard work. Resisting the temptations of television as much as the opportunities to go out with her friends once in a while had not been easy for a girl who was essentially a very sociable type. Looking proudly at her results, though, Susan felt that it had been all worth while, and that now she had earned a bit of easing off before the next effort of "A" levels.

In the Autumn term of Susan's Lower Sixth year, her friends teased her that she was trying to work through as many "serious" affairs with boys as most people had crowded into the two preceding years. Susan seemed incapable of taking her pleasures lightly, and declared herself truly in love with four different boys in a row—each of whom she had discarded after only a few weeks.

By the following March, though, just before the Easter holidays, Susan had settled down into what seemed a longer-lasting relationship. She and Don had been going steadily together for two months, and she told all her friends that they were going to get engaged. Her marks in the end-of-term exams were dreadful, and her teachers began to worry seriously about her university chances.

Susan's favourite teacher was the maths. teacher, Miss King. She was very upset when Miss King had a long talk with her at the beginning of the Summer term, and told her that unless she started some very hard work she would lose her chances of university altogether.

"You've wasted two-thirds of the year already, Susan," she pointed out, "and that is more than a third of the time you have altogether before 'A' levels. Next term you'll be sending in your application form, and getting your interviews. There is no time to waste if you really are serious about a university career. I think you have the makings of a first-class mathematician. Are you going to let this go to waste?"

Susan vowed that she would settle down to some hard work on the spot. She worked non-stop all that term, and by the summer holidays the affair with Don was completely dead, and she had pulled herself back up to a respectable level in her examinations.

The first term of her Upper Sixth year was completely taken up with applications, interviews, and school work. To her delight, just before Christmas she heard that she had been given a place at her second-choice university, provided she got the right "A" level passes. Her teachers congratulated her, and assured her that there was no reason why she should not get the right gradings in her exams—always, of course, providing that she worked well the next five months.

During the Christmas holidays, Susan met a young man who was studying for his final degree year as a member of a military college. His name was Frank, and he was a young lieutenant. He and Susan fell in love almost at first sight. Susan told him that it was like coming home after a very rocky voyage—she just felt "right" when she was with Frank, and nothing else seemed to matter much.

The two young people made plans in the following months. Frank would have his degree by July, so they fixed the following Christmas, just before Susan's nineteenth birthday, as the date for their wedding. By then, Frank would know what his posting was going to be, and Susan would have had a few months in which to get a job and save some money before the wedding. Susan's parents were disappointed at her decision to throw away her university plans, but they liked Frank, and felt that Susan had the right to make her own decisions.

The only cloud on Susan's sky was her future in-law's refusal to accept the idea. They felt that Frank was too young to know his own mind, and would spoil his own career chances by his involvement with Susan. They were shocked when they learned that Susan had only been seventeen when she and Frank met, and tried to persuade Frank to wait until Susan had got her own degree, and done three more years of growing up.

No-one, not even Susan, could pretend that her schoolteachers would be pleased at her sudden change of plans, and so she decided to say nothing at school, at least for a while. It distressed her when she was with Miss King, as she felt that she was in some way being dishonest, especially as Miss King thought she was getting exam. nerves, and gave her all sorts of extra help, and encouragement, in an effort to get her work up to scratch.

In fact, Susan and Frank drifted through the spring and early summer in a total haze. They spent every spare moment together, talking over their future plans, and speculating on how wonderful life together would be. June came, and they each faced their separate examinations—Finals for Frank, and "A" levels for Susan. No sooner were they over, than Susan left school and found a job in an office, intending to save towards their future home.

At the end of July, Frank went home to his parents for his annual long leave. Susan continued in her job, and told him to do all he could to persuade his parents that she wasn't about to ruin him.

While Frank was away, Susan found herself thinking about her future in realistic terms for the first time in months. Not until she was actually in an unskilled clerical job did she begin to realize just how she hated this sort of life. She felt all her interests and conversation had to be hidden from the other girls and women in the office, as she caught them making faces behind her back if she used long words, or expressed her opinions too forthrightly. They clearly thought she was "showing off." The prospect of condemning herself to a lifetime like this terrified her suddenly.

"What about the women who did go on to university, and made careers?" she asked herself. "Shall I be able to mix with them, and understand their ideas and thoughts, in five years time?" Her thoughts turned more and more to her career plans of the past few years. All the years of study and hard work that she had put in, before the time-wasting of the past two terms, how could she ever have contemplated throwing all that away?

For the last time, Susan felt that she was really seeing things clearly. She wrote to Frank and told him that she was breaking off their engagement. When he immediately returned to ask her face to face what was going on, she found herself still able to be firm.

"It isn't because I don't love you, Frank," she told him patiently, "it's just that I can't give up my own career plans. Your parents are right—I am only eighteen, and I need more time to grow up as myself, and find where I'm going in life, before I hitch my waggon to yours. I'd bore you stiff in a few years if I dropped everything just to be with you now."

At last Frank was convinced, and they agreed to remain friends, but to forget all wedding plans for a few years. Actually, Susan found herself impatient now with Frank, and didn't really want to see him any more. All her hopes and thoughts were centred on the results of her "A" levels, which would arrive any day through the post. If only, she prayed, the results had not been too badly affected by her stupid involvement with Frank during the last weeks before the exams.

Unfortunately, Susan's good fortune had deserted her. The results arrived, and she had done so badly that any thought of a university place was clearly impossible. Frank, too, received his results. He had failed to get his degree.

Questions for Discussion

1 Why did Susan have so many love-affairs during her first term in the Lower Sixth?

2 What do you think is really the reason for Susan's constant changes of heart?

3 Was the feeling Susan had for Don any different from the feeling she had for Frank?

4 Should a girl continue with her career plans, even after she has met the man she intends to marry?

5 Was there anywhere Susan could have turned for guidance in her decisions about marriage-or-career?

6 Do you think Frank's parents' proposal, that they should wait three years, was unreasonable?

7 Now that Susan has nothing but some very poor "A" level results, in maths. and science, what careers are open to her?

8 Do you agree with Susan's feelings about an unskilled clerical job?

Fred changes his Job

As the last note of the five o'clock hooter died slowly away, the long moving line of machine parts in Shop No. 4 came to a halt, and everywhere in the factory machines stopped. Men were reaching for their jackets and haversacks. It was Friday night, pay night, and time to go home.

For young Fred Simpson, this was the fourth Friday night that he'd lined up for his pay on this job. It was good pay as well, and when he went on the line in two years time, it would be very good—better than many skilled men could earn even in a good week. But you had to get to know the line before you really went on it. That was one of the reasons

68

why being a tea-boy was so important, although there was a lot more to it than that, and anybody who thought there wasn't a lot of responsibility in it just didn't know the score.

It was a tea-boy's job to look after men already working on the line. From the moment a man came on to the shop floor in the morning and took his place on the line he couldn't turn his back on it, until it stopped, not even for a minute, so that he depended on a boy, like Fred, to get him his tea and fetch him a packet of cigarettes whenever he needed them. Each man had to provide his own cup, and it was the boy's job to look after the cup and wash it up when he'd finished it. But a good boy could do a lot more things than that for a man. When a boy was experienced enough and could see what had to be done on the line, a man could step out for a few minutes and let his boy take over. When some of the older men in their middle and late thirties were getting tired, the only way they could carry on, sometimes, was to rely on a good boy being able to step in. Fred hadn't had to do this yet, but he was sure he'd be O.K. when he was asked.

It was all very different from the job he'd had when he first left school nearly twelve months ago. His father had apprenticed him to an electrician, and he'd liked the job at first. It was a change from school for one thing. Looking back, he hadn't hated school. In fact the last year had been not bad at all. He had been interested in science for one thing, and of all the teachers he remembered with any affection, Morrisey, the science teacher, stood out. They'd rebuilt an old car with Morrisey, just out of bits and pieces, and one of the best moments in that last year had been when they started it up and found it worked. They'd spent the whole of the double period pushing it and driving it around the school field. Fred had helped Morrisey with some of the electrical wiring and supposed this was why he'd decided to become an electrician really. Old Morrisey was all right.

Fred lined up for his pay packet. He had money in his pocket already. Men on the line tipped well. Even for fetching a packet of cigarettes a boy was tipped.

"Going down the rink, tonight, Fred?" asked one of his mates.

"May do," said Fred. "Depends what the bird says."

Fred had a girl. She was not exactly a steady date, but he liked to feel that she might be when he was talking to his mates, particularly those who'd been working longer than he had.

He collected his pay, then stopped to light a cigarette before he went to get his bike. The day he had enough for a down payment he was going to have a motor-cycle.

It was funny about his first job, really. He'd liked messing about with bits of wire and switches, but nobody had ever told him how lonely it could get, just working with one man and nobody else about of his own age. The electrician had been O.K. he supposed, but he never spoke to him very much, except to explain things on the job occasionally. All that winter they'd been working on a building site. He could still shiver when he remembered the cold. Why hadn't somebody said that electricians work out of doors even in winter? He hated working outside and hated being cold most of all. Nobody tells you nothing though. His teachers might have done, but they hadn't. Being fair, perhaps even old Morrisey didn't know. Still he'd stuck the job until the spring when it had done nothing but rain, and half the time he would get home wet to the skin.

At that point he'd remembered that once in the last year at school a woman had come from the local factory and had talked about the kind of jobs there were for boys like himself who were just about to leave school. She'd a pretty posh sort of accent, and the way she'd talked it sounded as though only the really smart boys would even get a look in on the jobs which were likely to be going. Anyhow, even by then,

Fred had been pretty set on becoming an electrician, and it wasn't until the following Spring that he remembered her again. He had thought about it a lot. Then one day, when it was raining buckets outside he'd made up his mind, and he'd put on his best suit and gone down to the factory where eventually he'd been directed to an office marked "Personnel."

He'd known her as soon as he saw her again. She looked quite sympathetic when he told her why he'd come, really quite nice. But she wasn't sure about a job for him. Jobs were pretty scarce right now and she wasn't at all certain that she would be able to offer him anything. He would have to fill in a form and she would let him know. He went home and changed into his working gear and went back to work with the electrician. Fred heard nothing more for three days, then when he came home in the evening, there was a letter addressed to Mr. F. C. Simpson. He still had the letter in his bedroom somewhere. It was typed in a very business-like way, but mainly it said that he had got the job and could start on the following Monday at eight o'clock.

He remembered that he'd gone wild with excitement. He waved the letter. "They're taking me, mom. They're really having me." His father had been a bit down, but he'd perked up before the end of the evening. "If it's what you really want, lad . . ."

Fred walked across the factory yard towards his bike. It was what he really wanted. He liked the rest of the lads. It was a good Company, and the men were O.K. too. It was a pretty easy job as well. A piece of cake if you kept your eyes open. Being an electrician was a hard job—a lot to learn and then you earned nothing to speak of. He'd watched the company electricians working sometimes. They never spoke to him. They wouldn't have even if they'd known him. Who'd catch an electrician talking to a line man? Sometimes he wished there was something to learn on a line, something really hard. But there wasn't. You just had to keep your eyes open and you'd be O.K.

Fred got on his bike and cycled out into the main stream of the factory traffic. He had money in his pocket, and maybe he'd be going out with his bird tonight. Life was O.K. and he felt fine.

Questions for Discussion

1 Why do you think Fred became an electrician's apprentice?

2 From what you know about Fred's job, what do you imagine might be some of its advantages? What might be some of its disadvantages?

3 How did Fred really feel about his job?

4 If you were choosing a job, how would you go about finding out whether it was the right one for you?

5 Make a list of all the people who could advise you about getting a job?

6 Make a list of questions you would want to ask a future employer before you took a job.

7 Some people say that the most important part of any job is what they call "job satisfaction." Discuss what you think is meant by this, and arrange a list, in order of importance, of the things which you think would bring "job satisfaction" to you.

Ann's Engagement

Ann Simpkin left her grammar school when she was fifteen, with only two "O" levels and a reputation amongst her teachers for being a difficult pupil. She herself was very relieved to get away from school. Although she had passed her 11-plus exam. well, and been very proud to get into the grammar school, she decided she hated it right from the very first term. Ann's sister had also been at the school—and also left at fifteen—and Ann felt that the teachers expected her to be one of the "bad girls" of the school, just because her sister had been.

After Ann had been at the school only six weeks, the Headmistress singled her out from the junior girls in front of the whole school during Assembly, and sent her to go and comb her hair. She said, "Girls with frizzy perms shouldn't be allowed into morning prayers, and no girl in this school is to come with her hair back-combed." Ann's hair was naturally curly, and she had washed it the night before. She always felt dreadfully self-conscious about the way it frizzed out after she washed it, and she had certainly never back-combed it in her life.

From then on, Ann's school life became a long battle with teachers for some measure of independence in dress. She was convinced that some teachers looked for faults in her school uniform which they would have ignored in others. On one awful day, she had to go to school in a yellow blouse of her mother's, because her four-year-old brother spilt his milk all over her last clean white blouse at breakfast. Her form-teacher never gave her any chance to explain, she simply sent her straight home to change, and told her not to come back into school until she was properly dressed. Ann's mother was dreadfully upset when Ann arrived home in angry tears, and she herself went straight off on the bus to see the Headmistress. Although the Head was quite pleasant, and said she was sorry there had been a mix-up, she still told Mrs. Simpkin that she thought the whole family had a bad attitude to the school. She also made Mrs. Simpkin very angry, by saying that she thought that life over the family business, by which she meant the snack-bar run by Mr. and Mrs. Simpkin together, was "most unsuitable for a young girl." Ann quite enjoyed living over the snack-bar, though she was determined not to work there when she left school, as her sister did.

As the school years went by, Ann found herself longing for the time when she could leave school. At one time she had thought of being a nurse, but she decided that the training might be too much like the Girl's Grammar atmosphere all over again. She talked things over with her parents, and they encouraged her to take a course at the Technical College in Catering. She sat for four "O" levels, and passed in English and Dressmaking, failing both History and English Literature. Then she escaped with no regrets, out of school into what she thought of as the "real world."

Ann enjoyed her work in college, and made friends during the day with some of the girls on the same course. They spent most of their free time in the down-town coffee bars, often comparing notes about their families, and the lives of the older girls at the college. Ann often talked about her elder sister, who was in trouble at home because her parents disliked her new boy-friend. They had a tremendous row with him on one occasion and Ann told her friends all about it next day. Sometimes the girls went to the pictures together in the evenings, and a few of them had boy-friends to go out with. Ann used to help her parents in the snack-bar in the evenings, but always felt dreadfully tired by eight o'clock and often just went to bed by half-past eight, night after night.

By the time she was sixteen, Ann was smoking heavily, and often had bad headaches and dizzy turns. She still enjoyed her work at college, but only towards Christmas of that year did she finally meet a boy who was interested in her, and wanted to take her out regularly. She and Jeff spent all their free time together, usually just sitting talking in the Simpkins' snack-bar. After a few months, they clubbed together to buy an old car, and spent many evenings driving round in it.

Life seemed to Ann to drift aimlessy. She worried about

Jeff, who had no training at all, and moved from job to job every few weeks. In July, just before her seventeenth birthday, her sister dropped a bomb-shell. She was pregnant by the boy the family disliked, and was marrying him immediately. Ann's mother told Ann that she would have to give up her catering course, and come to work in the business. Ann left college, and she and Jeff got engaged on her seventeenth birthday.

Questions for Discussion

1 Why do you think Ann and her sister were labelled the "bad girls" of their grammar school?

2 Do you think Ann's attitude was in any way to blame for her position at school?

3 What do you think of the Headmistress's remark about life above a snack-bar?

4 What do you think are Ann's feelings towards her sister?

5 Why do you think Ann did so poorly in her "O" level examinations? Was there any way in which she could have acted more wisely in that year?

6 Was Ann's tiredness in the evenings a sign that she was working too hard, do you think?

7 What other career besides catering could Ann have thought about, with her qualifications and education?

8 Why did Ann get engaged to Jeff on her seventeenth birthday?

Bob's Revenge

Bob had lived on the Estate for most of his life. The fourth of a family of five, he had passed through the local primary school and then the county secondary school without impressing any of his teachers very favourably although never involving himself in any major trouble. At sixteen, he was still small for his age, with apparently little interest in girls, or, for that matter in anything except the Falcons.

The Falcons all came from the Estate, and as a gang ranged from fifteen-year-olds who had just left school that year to a few seventeen-year-old youths who were "king" Falcons. They all wore black leather jackets with Falcon insignia which they had chosen from a catalogue. They possessed a few motor-cycles and scooters among them, upon which the more privileged in the gang took turns to ride round the Estate, yelling and hooting as they went. Occasionally they would go down to the local youth club and jeer at those inside. Sometimes, they would congregate in the Estate's telephone kiosk and call up girls, although for most of them actual social contact with girls was very limited (although every one of them had detailed and lurid stories about girls they had met or been out with). They were essentially a boys' gang and were happy to leave it that way. Sometimes they would all go down to the nearest public house for a "booze up," although the landlord of the Estate pub usually refused to serve them as a group as he was well aware that most of them were under age.

Bob had become one of the Falcons as soon as he had left school. He had saved up for his jacket and had bought it after only two months with a "loan" from his mother. He was very proud of it and wore it all the time whenever he was out. He now longed for the day when he would be able to have a motor-cycle.

Bob was not the most popular of the Falcons. He had always been a quiet, rather morose boy, who cried easily when he was hurt, and in school he could never be completely depended upon to stay quiet if there was any trouble with the teachers brewing. As a youngster he had invariably had a runny nose, and his classmates had early on nicknamed him "Snotty," a name which had stuck even when he had joined the Falcons. But he was useful in the gang and he always seemed to have money to spend. He also added to the gang's numbers, which was important to them whenever they wanted to make their presence felt down town.

One particular Saturday afternoon they all decided to go to the local park. This was a favourite haunt of young people who could lie, usually unmolested, on the grass, and eat ice-cream, or kick a ball about. There was also a boating pond where it was always possible to fool around, rocking boats or ramming one another in the shallow, dirty water. If one of the park keepers came up, they would laugh and jeer at him, although rarely did one of them approach them now, so they felt that the Falcon reputation was well established.

On this afternoon, they suddenly saw a small group of girls sitting on the grass. They were all girls from the Estate.

"Ey, Gladys, going out tonight, are you?" one of the boys yelled.

"Mind your own business, Arty Jones," replied the girl in a tone which was meant to be frosty.

"Ey, she knows your name, Arty? Good old Arty. Bet she's hot stuff, Arty." By this time, the little group of girls was surrounded by the boys. The girls looked at one another, still trying to preserve their dignity with these boys whom they had known for years, but being a little frightened by the black jackets and jeering faces.

"You think you're so big, you lot. Why don't you go back to your moms," said one of the girls. Just then, one of the boys pushed one of the girls. "Oh stop it, you silly ——" the girl said. "Why don't you —— well grow up."

"Language, language!" the boys jeered. One of the girls tried to push her way out. The others tried to follow.

"Not so fast, not so fast," and one of the "king" Falcons, a tall seventeen year old, caught one of the girls by her arm. "Let go of me, you stupid ——" yelled the girl, and she hit him with her handbag. The next moment, there was a real mix-up, the boys shoving and pushing, the girls in the middle of it, screaming, kicking and biting.

At the beginning Bob had been on the outside of the group, laughing and jeering at the girls' obvious embarrassment. When the mix-up began, he found himself struggling with one of the smaller girls—a girl who lived a few doors away from him, called Millie. "Leave go of me, you snotty-nosed ——" screamed the girl. Bob grappled with her even more, trying to pin her to the ground. She hit him over the ear, then brought up her knee into his groin with all her force. The pain was awful. It seemed to well up inside him and spread like fire through his whole body. He must have blacked out for a few seconds, because the next thing he knew he was sitting holding his stomach and retching agonizingly. Everybody else seemed to be running away.

Bob's mother took him to the hospital where he spent three days "under observation," being X-rayed and examined to ensure that there was no internal injury. For most of this time he ached and felt sick. All he could think about was the girl Millie and how he could get even with her. He would hurt her as she had hurt him, and would laugh and laugh and laugh . . . . If only he could get her on her own, if only for a minute, he'd make her pay.

The first night he was home, it was raining and there were no Falcons. He didn't go to work next day, but lay on the sofa reading his brother's comics. He felt bored. Then he thought about Millie and how he was going to get her. By the time his two elder brothers had come home in the evening, he had thought up his plan.

"Hey, Dave. Will you lend me your air-pistol?" he said.

"What, for you to shoot yourself with? Or me, likely. Not on your life. You get your own air-pistol," and his brother went on with his tea.

But Bob was not to be put off. Next morning, after Dave had gone to work and the house was empty, Bob crept up to his brother's room, and after a search found the pistol among a pile of clothing. With it was a small box of lead pellets. He pushed the pistol and the pellets into his pocket. "Now I've got you, you —— you."

Millie was still at school and he watched through the window all that week. He saw her coming home each day, but she was usually with a crowd of her friends. Once he nearly caught her alone, but she saw him and ran. Then, on Friday his chance came. About five o'clock he saw her go to the telephone box, pick up the phone and begin dialling. He walked out of the house and towards the box. Her back was towards him and she was so busy talking that she didn't see him. He waited against the wall outside. At last, after what seemed an interminable age, she put down the phone and turned to come out. She saw him then. She hesitated, then decided to put a bold front on it and pushed open the door of the box and stepped out.

"Hello," she smiled weakly. "You O.K. now, are you?"

Bob felt the butt of the pistol underneath his coat. "You ——" he said. He felt himself beginning to cry. "I'll get you now, you ——"

Millie stared at him. Then she began to run.

"Wait!" he shouted. He had pulled out the pistol. He raised it and pressed the trigger. There was no recoil, no sound other than the "poof" of air. He saw Millie falter and clutch her arm. Then she was screaming.

He looked at the pistol, then threw it into the bushes, and began to run towards his house. He was crying as he ran.

Questions for Discussion

1 Why do you think Bob joined the Falcons?

2 Do gangs like the Falcons serve any real purpose for anybody?

3 Do you think that Millie was right in using as much force as she obviously did in the "horseplay" in the park?

4 Do you think that the "fight" between the Falcons and the girls was really intended? Was there any way in which it could have been prevented?

5 If you were approached by a group such as the Falcons, what would you do?

6 Apart from the fact that he had been hurt, why do you think that Bob felt so deeply about his revenge?

7 How do you think Bob felt after the shooting? Do you think that he would really feel that he had his revenge?

A Police-Raid at the Party

Most people would agree that Mr. Wilford was the best kind of father anyone could wish for. He had been Headmaster of one of the city's most successful secondary modern schools for seven years, and was well-known and liked throughout the city. Both his daughters went to the mixed grammar school, although Carol, the elder, had been offered a place at the girl's direct grant grammar school. Mr. Wilford, however, believed that co-education was better for young people, and privately, too, he wanted to avoid making too great a distinction between the clever Carol and her much slower younger sister Grace.

The two sisters were as different as two girls from the same family could possibly be. Physically, Carol was small and fair like her mother, while Grace was tall and dark like her father. Grace was outgoing, and friendly, while Carol, though cheerful and well-liked, was much shyer, and slower to make friends than her sister. Her marks were consistently high, and academically there was no doubt that she would leave her younger sister far behind.

Mr. Wilford was a forceful man, with a loud laugh, and a masculine, outdoors kind of personality. Within his own home, there was no doubt that he was the absolute boss, and while he was unquestionably a loving father and a home-loving man those who knew the Wilfords well often wondered how his wife could put up with his bossiness towards her. Carol, although she admired her father, and envied his easy, casual manner with large social groups, still decided that she would never get trapped into the sort of subservient position that her mother had been forced to occupy.

Carol liked to do well at school, but wanted even more to be popular, and have a well-known name in the school, like Grace. Grace, at fourteen, had far more boy-friends than Carol had at sixteen. Every week-end, Grace would come home and beg her father for permission to go to two or more parties on Friday and Saturday nights, while Carol rarely went anywhere more exciting than shopping with a girl-friend, or once or twice to the pictures with a boy called Ted, who bored her stiff, and whom she had known since they were both at the sand-pit age.

In her fifth year in secondary school, Carol found herself, to her delight, being approached several times, in a friendly fashion, by some of the other, more popular girls in her form. She wondered afterwards, after the scandal, whether they were only interested in her because the teachers thought she was "respectable," and so conferred respectability on the other girls. At first, though, she basked in this unexpected limelight, and was deeply flattered when she was invited to one of their Saturday parties.

After two or three parties, Carol was left in no doubt that not only were several of the boys bringing in beer and even spirits to the parties, without the adults in the house knowing it, but she also began to realize that some of the "cigarettes" being passed around were "reefers" or, as she had called them when she had spoken in her form debate, marijuana. She had argued, in that debate, that the laws against "soft" drugs should be abolished, and that young people should be allowed to smoke "pot" when they wanted, at the age when they were old enough to know what they were doing. Carol was a little shaken, though, to discover how very different the whole question seemed when it was really happening, not just a subject for school debate.

Lying awake after the third such party, Carol tried to reason with herself about the problem as she saw it. First, she had to admit that the sheer fear of what would happen if they were caught breaking the law, was her major concern. Even though there seemed little chance of its happening, it was not a pleasant thought.

Secondly, she realized that the change in behaviour and personality which occurred in the boys and girls she knew, when they were under the influence of the drug, was most unpleasant. Vaguely, it reminded Carol of one Christmas when she was a child, and one of her uncles had got very drunk, and had ceased to seem like her dear Uncle John any longer. The shock of finding a stranger behind a familiar face had long remained with her, and she hated it now in her friends, as she had all those years ago.

Set against these arguments was the fact that Carol had publicly declared, in the debate, that she was "for" soft drugs, and that she enjoyed the feeling of being accepted in the conspiratorial atmosphere of the parties. She wasn't, after all, she reminded herself, involved in taking drugs herself, and therefore, she believed, she was not breaking the law. The alternative, to withdraw from the parties, would mean that she would lose these new friendships, and that she did not want to do.

For one brief moment, Carol allowed herself to think of the possibility of telling her mother what was happening at the parties. She abandoned the idea immediately. Without doubt, her mother would tell her father, and that was quite unthinkable. He would rush to the police, and want her to tell him the names of every single person involved. No, better forget the whole thought of involving her mother, she reflected.

As the term went by, Carol found that although her worry about drug-taking amongst her friends was still with her during the week, and affecting her work at school, no doubt, yet at week-ends, she was enjoying the parties more and more. One boy, Stephen, seemed to be particularly attracted to her, and although he also never took the reefers that were passed around, he used to argue with her that it was really the law that was stupid, and that they were really just making a stand for their right to do what they felt was reasonable and sensible.

The last week of term, before Easter, Carol and Stephen went together to a party at the house of one of the wildest, and, to Carol, the least sensible, of all the boys in the gang. This boy, whom they all called Jack, drank heavily at all the parties, was their source of supply for the reefers, and hated all adults with a deep hatred. His mother was away for the week-end—his parents were divorced—and so they had the house completely to themselves. Not surprisingly, the party became very rowdy, and for the first time in months, Carol found herself genuinely panicking at the situation.

"Stephen, take me home," she begged. "This is just horrid." She thought of her parents, and suddenly saw the whole party with her father's eyes. It was frightening. Stephen was a little too drunk to hear the panic in her voice.

"Come on, Carol, there's nothing to worry about," he replied with a silly grin.

Carol had actually gone into the bedroom, to search for her coat under the pile of bodies lying on the bed, when the knocking came at the door. Afterwards, she could not even remember what had happened during the hour that followed. The police had entered the house, and taken them all down to the police station. Many of the young people were too "high" on drugs, or too drunk, to realize what was happening to them.

After what seemed like years, their parents had gradually started to arrive at the police station, and eventually they were allowed home, one by one. Carol was beyond feeling anything but intense relief at the sight of her parents' familiar faces, when she saw them come through the door. Wordlessly, they took her home, and her mother helped her into bed.

The next day, all the people at the party were in court. Carol, like most of the others, was given a suspended sentence. Her parents were in court, and as she stood up to receive her sentence, Carol looked at her father's face. "He looks like an old, old man," she thought to herself. "I'm sorry, Daddy, I never meant to hurt you as much as that."

Questions for Discussion

1 Can you form any idea of what Carol's feelings towards her parents were?

2 Why did Carol continue at the parties, even when she found out that they involved drugs?

3 Would things have been better if Carol had told her mother about the parties?

4 What do you think of Carol's arguments to herself "for" and "against" the taking of marijuana amongst her friends?

5 Do you think that Carol has behaved selfishly towards her family?

6 What sort of boy is Jack?

7 How much do you know about the laws relating to drugs?

The Stolen Cigarettes

Bill was the second of three boys. His elder brother Frank was twenty-five, grown up and gone away to sea, but his younger brother, John, was thirteen, two years younger than he was himself.

The family had always moved around a fair amount. Bill's father had been wounded fighting the Japs in 1941, and had been a prisoner-of-war, as well. Bill thought his father was a great hero, and didn't in the least mind hearing stories of the far-off days of 1939 and 1940, and his Dad's life in the Jap camp. Frank had been less kind about his father, and before he left home there had been a great row, which Bill could still remember, in which Frank had told his father that he was lazy and no good to anyone.

Bill's father did have trouble keeping a job—largely because of his health, as he often explained. However, the family had stayed for six years—from Bill's eighth birthday until he was fourteen—in the same large Midland city. Bill liked the city. He liked the school he went to, that is, he liked the boys he made his friends there, and there was always plenty to do in the evenings—cinemas, coffee-bars, a bowling alley, skating rink, and Saturday dances for those old enough or brave enough to want to go.

When the family moved to a small town when Bill was fourteen, he was very disappointed. One of the great attractions of the city had been the fact that he could build up a really nice bit of income from a big paper round. When he first moved away, he found himself desperately short of cash for cigarettes and for the new clothes that he had liked to wear when out with his mates. His first efforts to get any work at his age in Smalltown were totally unsuccessful.

However, just after Christmas he managed to get a paper round in Smalltown which paid him 32s. 6d. a week. This was fine and he was now able to flash his money around in school and in the coffee bar as he'd done before. Then just before Easter he got himself involved with a girl. It wasn't that Bill felt very much towards Diane, but she was an attractive girl, and being seen taking her out made him

85

feel pretty big. Sometimes they went to the pictures together, and occasionally to a Saturday evening dance. The trouble was that the money from the paper round wasn't really enough any more.

The newspaper shop for which Bill worked was also a tobacconist's, and it seemed fairly easy for him to take the occasional packet of cigarettes without the owner noticing it immediately. In any case, Bill was not the only newspaper boy, and he had worked out that if the owner ever found out he would never be able to pin it on him. Originally, taking the occasional packet had meant that he hadn't had to spend so much money on cigarettes. But now, with money really short, he decided to take even more, as he knew there was a ready market for cigarettes among some of his friends and acquaintances at school. It was this that eventually trapped him. Bill already had a bad reputation at school among the teachers. His work in class was slipshod and he was always in trouble of some sort or other. He had been caught smoking several times, and it was on one of these occasions, when the master on duty had found a group of boys smoking behind the football pavilion, that the source of the cigarette supply had come to light. Exactly how many cigarettes Bill had taken over the period it was difficult to say, but the tobacconist stated that since January, he had been unable to account for well over fifteen pounds' worth of his stock.

In Juvenile Court, Bill found himself on probation. He was, of course, now without his paper round, and Diane was now going around with someone else. When she met him she just passed him by as though he'd never existed. At school things seemed worse than ever. He had become truculent and even the most patient of his teachers admitted that he was quite a handful. No-one at home was much help. All his mother had done since the police had come to the house was cry and blame him for the disgrace he'd brought

86

on his family. His father had sworn at him when it first happened and had knocked him across the kitchen. John wasn't bad, but John never did say very much. After the day in Court, they were lying in bed in the room they shared together.

"What was it like?" asked John.

"Oh, all right." Bill replied. "They're just a lot of silly b's." Then he said, "I'm sick of this place. When this term's over I'm leaving, like Frank. Silly old b's, I'll show them."

"Where'll you go?"

"I'm going to sea, that's what I'm doing."

Much later, John awoke. It was still dark, and he thought he could hear Bill crying. But he went back to sleep, and next morning he thought he must have dreamed it.

Questions for Discusssion

1 Why do you think Bill did so badly at school? Was he really a "bad lot"?

2 What do you think that Bill really thought about his parents? Why?

3 Why did Bill think it was so important to have money?

4 If you had been in John's position, was there any way in which you could have helped Bill?

5 Do you think that John really dreamed that his brother was crying?

6 What do you think about Bill's idea of going away to sea? Do you think this would solve any of his problems?

7 If you were unfortunately in Bill's position, what would you do?

8 From what you have learned about Bill, what might you predict about his future? What kind of man do you think he will become?

Angela

The girls who knew Angela always said that her boy-craze started when she was sixteen, after she had lived in the south-west for two years. Their parents, however, tended to blame Angela's wildness on the fact that she had grown up in Birmingham, which they regarded as a big, tough city where anything could happen.

Angela's father was considerably older than her mother, and was the perfect image of the successful Birmingham business man. He was proud of being self-made, and both indulged and adored his daughter, from the time she was born. Angela's mother often said that Angela could twist her father round her little finger—nothing was too good for her, including a personal spending allowance which was about ten times larger than anything any other girl of her acquaintance could hope to see.

Despite his indulgent attitude towards his daughter, Mr. Brown and Angela had occasional monumental rows, when he would shout at her in a fury, and tell her she was no good. Since his retirement to Devon these rows had become worse, although Mrs. Brown could not decide whether this was because Angela had reached a more self-assertive age or because her father had less now to occupy his thoughts.

The girls and boys with whom Angela went to school were a little in awe of her on the whole. The boys were afraid to ask her out, because she seemed so worldly-wise, and they were afraid she would laugh at them. The girls admired her beautiful clothes, and liked to be invited to the Brown's new house, full of modern gadgets, as well as their huge yacht moored in the bay just a few miles away.

It was in the summer after Angela's sixteenth birthday that the others watched the boy-craze get into full swing.

Angela met a crowd of summer visitors, mostly young boys of nineteen or more, who parked their mini-bus in the lane near the Brown's house and made friendly advances when Angela spoke to their group.

The local young people dismissed this kind of group as mad summer visitor type, but Angela thought they were wonderful, and dropped all her friends in order to spend every moment with the new boys. Three of the boys were an aspiring musical group, and Angela declared them to be the most wonderful musicians she had ever heard. She persuaded her father to ask some of his friends to hire the group for parties and dances, so that they would stay all summer.

When that summer came to an end, Angela was a different person. All she talked, dreamed, or thought, were her pop-group friends. She bought every record she could lay hands on, and played them all day, because, she said, you had to be in touch with the very latest sounds if you were to develop your style just right. She told her friends that she was going to be the group's manager one day, because she had the same business-sense as her father.

People began to gossip seriously when Angela twice ran away in the middle of the week, to go to be with her musical friends and hear them play. Her parents had forbidden her to go to them, and she and her father had had such a terrible row that Mrs. Brown began to fear for his heart. Angela taunted her father by telling him that she had slept with all the group, and with "dozens" of their friends as well. "That's just the way it is for a girl on the pop-scene, Daddy," she said with tolerant superiority. "You just have to put out to get accepted."

Her parents were above all determined to avoid taking police action about their daughter. Although her habit of disappearing from home became more and more frequent, her mother always knew that she would come back as soon as the group tired of her, and her money ran out, so she preferred to say nothing, and hope that Angela would grow out of the craze. She pinned her hopes on the thought that Angela might meet a boy locally who could engage her interest and keep her at home.

In fact, Angela was not really very interested in the experience of going to bed with boys. As she had so cruelly told her father, it had been demanded of her as the price of acceptance in the group's life, but it had all happened too casually, and without any feeling, for her, of a real affection for any one person. She had learned to ignore the experience of sex, do what was required of her, and forget all about it. Indeed, she found herself less and less able really to think about what she was doing these days. She had the feeling sometimes that she was living in a dream, and nothing she did or said was real.

The only time Angela seemed to get upset now was when she returned from one of her trips and saw how distressed her father had been. She had stopped the pretence of going to school, and her father had offered to help her towards any job in the world she chose, or to let her just stay at home, and perhaps travel, the three of them together. Angela really was fond of her parents, and she tried to make them understand how much her friends meant to her, and how important she felt the group were destined to become, if only she could help them more. On this topic, though, there was just no point of contact. Her parents could not and would not understand about her feelings for the group. They were determined to make her break her connections there.

Matters got worse over the next few months. Angela was invited once more to a local party of young people, and she got drunk, with some gin she had brought herself, and then persuaded one of the young boys from her old school to go to bed with her, upstairs in the parents' bedroom. All the village knew about it, it seemed, by the next day. Angela's lack of popularity with her own age-group also meant that they did not feel any obligation to keep quiet to their elders about her wrong-doings.

After one long absence from home of three weeks, during which her parents had had two telephone calls, to prevent them sending the police to look for her, Angela arrived home late one evening looking very miserable, dirty and unkempt. She told her mother she wasn't feeling well, and went straight to bed.

Mrs. Brown called for their doctor, who came the next morning. When he had seen Angela alone in her bedroom for a few minutes, he called Mrs. Brown into the room.

"Angela knows what I am going to tell you, and she has agreed that you should know, Mrs. Brown," he began. "I'm very much afraid that Angela has a form of venereal disease. Now, don't get too upset—it can be cured, although I think it has been going on for some months. But I have been telling Angela that from now on she will have to change her way of life—for the sake of others and herself."

Afterwards Mrs. Brown could hardly remember what she said, while the doctor tried to explain the treatment Angela would require. Angela was crying hysterically whilst the doctor was talking, and she continued to cry after he had gone.

When her mother finally calmed her down, she said, "Mummy, please forgive me. I'll stay at home, and be a good daughter to you and Daddy for the rest of my life. Only please, please, don't tell Daddy this!"

Questions for Discussion

1 Do you think Angela's parents are to blame for the way she grew up?

2 How do you think Angela felt towards the boys and girls in her country school?

3 Why did the group of young musicians and their friends seem so wonderful to Angela?

4 Why did the experience of sex mean so little to Angela?

5 Were Angela's parents right to try to break her connection with the group? Do you think there is any way they could have succeeded?

6 What sort of venereal disease do you think Angela has got? What treatment will she need, and how will it affect her?

7 What future life do you think Angela will plan for herself now?

The Boy who was Interviewed

Behind Milton Secondary School there was a winding road through the trees, where the schoolboys often took a short cut at the end of the day. At the end of the normal school day the road was, therefore, fairly well-used, but an hour later, as Roger came out of the science labs, it was quite deserted and growing dark in the waning autumn light.

Roger had been working late several evenings on his science project for the school's science fair. He was very interested in all things mechanical, and apt to lose himself completely in work which he was allowed to pursue on his own initiative. At fourteen, though, Roger found interest in few activities at school. He was slow to develop, small for his age, and suffered from having been born with fair, curly hair, and long eyelashes that had earned him teasing from his school-friends all his life. His embarrassment at his childish appearance had made him more than normally shy during the past year, and he had developed the habit of withdrawing from the gang of his previous friends, and spending much of his time alone.

As he walked back, hurrying slightly to be home before dark, he noticed for the third evening in succession that a large, rather expensive car was drawn up at the side of the lane through the woods. This time, however, the man opened the door of the car and stepped out as he saw Roger approaching.

"Excuse me," he said, in an educated, though slightly hesitant manner, "I wonder if I could have a word with you for a minute?"

Roger stopped and looked surprised.

"Yes?" he replied.

The man then explained that he represented a national teenage T.V. programme, which was doing a survey of teenagers' interests in music, theatre, and cinema. He explained that it was his job to interview several teenagers about their taste in these fields, and asked if Roger would be willing to act as one of his "subjects" for the survey.

Roger felt flattered by being selected in this way as representative of the interests of the viewers of such a sophisticated programme as the one mentioned by the man. However, he felt that his parents would not take kindly to his staying out even later, so he apologized to the man, but explained that he would have to be getting home quickly.

"No need to worry about that," was the reassuring answer, "I can meet you here again tomorrow. Perhaps if you could be just half an hour earlier coming along we would have time for the interview without making you late home."

Roger readily agreed to this arrangement, and promised to meet the man at the same place at five o'clock the next afternoon. He went on home rather pleased with himself, thinking that the other boys would be envious when he told them that someone from their favourite programme had interviewed him.

Unfortunately, when Roger told his friends what had happened the next morning, they all howled with laughter. They refused to believe that he really had met someone from the television company, and they insisted that this just wasn't the way programme research was carried on. When

93

he continued to insist that he really had had the conversation he described, his friends told him that the man must be a "weirdie," as they described it. "He'll probably drag you off into the bushes and murder you horribly," suggested David, and this caused more howls of laughter as they imagined in lurid detail how poor Roger might meet his fate.

At last, one or two of the boys decided to take him halfway seriously. "Look, Titch," David said, "this sounds like the sort of man our mothers warned us about. If, and it's a big If, you are telling the truth, then, for heavens' sake, we'll hide in the bushes to see what happens, and DON'T, whatever you do, get into his car with him. Stay out, in full view, so we know what's going on."

Obviously only half convinced of the man's existence, three others agreed to keep watch from the bushes with David, when Roger went to keep his appointment.

As soon as school was finished, the four boys went off to take up their hiding place, telling Roger to wait twenty minutes, until just before five, and then come slowly along the path. Their disbelief and teasing made Roger angry, and he was greatly relieved to see, as he turned into the lane, that the man was indeed waiting for him as arranged.

"Hello, Roger," the man greeted him. "I'm glad you could come."

He then went on to say, laughing, that it seemed rather silly to stand out in the lane talking any longer. "I have the questionnaires in my briefcase," he continued. "Let's get into the car, and I'll read you the questions."

Once Roger was in the car, the man switched on the ignition and started up the engine. Roger, remembering now the warnings of his friends, asked him nervously where they were going. The man began to draw away from the roadside and the big car swung into the centre of the small lane. Before any more could be said, Roger's friends dashed out from the bushes, in clear view of the car's rear-view mirror.

"Are those some friends of yours?" asked the man, still quite friendly.

"Well, yes, some fellows from school. I noticed them as I came along to meet you," replied Roger, feeling out of his depth. "Where are you driving me?"

"Are you worried about something?" he was asked, and as the words were said, Roger could feel the atmosphere change, and for the first time he was worried, really worried. His intelligence began to work. The main thing, he decided, was to get across the idea that his friends were not as stupid as he had been, without frightening the man into any action which might be panic.

"Not worried, exactly," he said, with what he hoped was an open smile, "But my friends were kidding me about meeting you, and telling me not to go driving off with strange men." He waited for the answer, with his heart in his mouth.

"My word, they are men of the world, your friends, aren't they?" was the somewhat acid reply. There was complete silence for a moment. "Do you know, I think I'm having trouble with one of my tyres," the man said suddenly and very smoothly. "I think we'd better postpone our interview until tomorrow while I find a garage. Can you find your way if I drop you here?"

As the car stopped, Roger virtually jumped out. He began to walk back towards where he had last seen his friends. In fact, he had hardly gone a hundred yards before a police-car, summoned by David, swung round the corner looking for the big car. The police were obviously as suspicious of "the man" as was David, and they spoke some firm words to Roger about trusting strangers. He had to make a statement at the police station, and the police telephoned the television company, only to find that no survey was being undertaken amongst teenagers at all. When he thought it over Roger was very grateful to David after all.

Questions for Discussion

1 Why did Roger agree so readily to become a survey "subject"?

2 Do you think Roger was unusually stupid in agreeing to meet this man?

3 How could Roger have protected himself against an illegal "interview"? What would you do before agreeing to meet a stranger in a deserted lane?

4 What kind of person do you think this man really was? Are there many such people in the world?

5 Do you think Roger's friends had done the right thing in calling for the police, when Roger drove off in the car?

6 What did Roger do to make the man decide to let him out of the car?

7 Discuss some of the dangers that people can meet from other, disturbed human beings. How can these be best avoided? How can society help disturbed human beings to change their behaviour?

Dear Joan . . .

Sept. 19th.

Dear Joan,

Well, here I am, after two weeks of this HORRID new school. The girls here aren't a bit like us, they all go about in little cliques, and don't even want to know as far as a new girl is concerned. Pity poor old me.

The teachers aren't bad, that is, they aren't any worse than the lot at A.H.S., not that that's saying much. There's one other new girl this term besides me. Her name's Joyce, and she seems O.K. so far. She goes home on the same bus as me, as well, so I think we'll probably keep each other going for a bit. Actually, the school bus is the best part of the whole deal. We share it with the boys' school, and the mixed Grammar school, so there are thousands of boys, and only four girls. Mind you, those four include Annabel, same form as me at school, and marvellous figure, fantastic clothes. She's sixteen already, which makes me seem a babe in arms, still waiting hopefully for my fifteenth birthday. What boy is going to look at me with her around? ? ?

I don't dare ask what Malcolm has been up to since we moved. He wrote once, about three weeks ago, vowing eternal grief, etc., etc., but I expect Martha has consoled him by now. She was just waiting to pounce like the nasty cat she is.

Give my love to all the kids. I miss them. I even miss Mrs. James, believe it or not. The English mistress here is a real crab, even though she's quite young and not bad looking. She obviously doesn't think much of me, which is serious, since English was about my only hope for a decent grading in my O-levels. How are you doing with your Latin? Thank heaven I don't have that to worry about at least.

Please write soon and tell me everything, every single little thing. I'm already counting days to seeing you all when we come up for Christmas.

> Yours till the cows come home,
> Elizabeth.

Oct. 1st.

Dear Elizabeth,

It was lovely to hear all your news. Your mother has written to mine saying I can spend all August with you in the summer, did you know? ? ? Isn't it marvellous? Poor you with all those snooty girls. I do hope you've been able to get on a bit with them now, and Joyce sounds all right.

I haven't really been doing anything special since term started. The old place goes on much as before. The Allen sisters have sort of included me a bit in their doings, so I'm not too left out of things without you, though Drama Club is miserable these days. Mrs. James tries to cheer me up, and says I should throw myself into my acting, even without you there as a team, but there isn't anyone left who can see what a play is all about, and really thrash it out the way we got them to do when we both really worked on them. Martha thinks she is just the answer to prayer, of course, and wants to do "The Doll's House"—with her in the lead, need I add! As if she could! ! ! She hasn't bothered much with Malcolm since you weren't there to compete with. He still comes along to Drama, and he came to the Theatre with Mike and me the other night. I think he really is missing you, honest no kidding and for real.

Miss Houseman was asking about you the other day. She asked how you were liking an all girls' school, and I said I thought you were missing A.H.S. She sort of snorted, honestly, it was disgusting.

Mrs. Cross told me the other day that I might scrape a three in Latin if I worked hard! Can you believe that? My mother was so astonished I had to revive her with smelling salts practically.

Excuse the exercise paper, especially as your letter was on such beautiful stationery. I'm writing this in the chem. lab. Not in a chem. lesson I hasten to say. I've come in here in the lunch-hour, as Mike said he would try and finish his practice early. Some hope, it's too late now anyway.

Please write again soon.

Lots of love,

Joan.

October 12th.

Dear Joan,

I am half dying, honestly. I've been in bed all week with the most ghastly 'flu, and a terribly high temperature. I went to school on Monday, and felt simply awful all day. By the end of the day I felt too dreadful for words, and I thought I would never walk the last half mile home from the school bus. Then when I got home my mother was out, and I crawled into bed with all my clothes on. She didn't realize what was the matter, and told me to get up and put my pyjamas on, but I nearly collapsed on the floor, so she realized then, and had to help me to get my things off. I only hope I can get up before my birthday next week. There's this dishy boy on the bus, and he has asked me to go to the pictures with him next Saturday. I'll just die if I'm not well enough to go by then, honestly I will.

Tell Malcolm I'm still true to him, really I am. I have to go out sometimes, though, don't I?

Love from your poor dying friend,
Elizabeth.

October 17th

Dear Elizabeth,

I hope you're better now, you poor thing. Lots of people have had 'flu here, too. We had six of the form away all at once, and lots of the teachers have been ill, too.

The enclosed comes with much love, and best wishes for being fifteen at last. Fifteen has been a horrid year for me so far, I hope it's better for you, anyway. Let me know if you went out with the dishy boy.

Many happy returns,
Joan.

October 21st.

Dear Joan,

Thank you for the book token. I'll let you know when I have chosen something with it. You shouldn't have spent half your month's pocket money on my birthday present, though. I shall worry now about how you'll manage the rest of the month.

Well, I got up at the week-end, and staggered around. I went back to school on the Monday, and had a dreadful time catching up. They make you actually do all the written work you've missed, so I was up doing homework until nearly midnight every night. Isn't it an awful rule? By the time Saturday came I was jolly glad to go out with Tony, I can tell you. But the night was awful. I just can't bear to think about it.

He was so sweet, and came and said hello to my parents first and everything, and I could tell he'd made a good impression, especially on my Father. We saw the film, which ended at quarter past ten, and my parents had told me I was to get home by eleven at the latest. Well, just as we were coming out of the cinema, we met Annabel (fab. clothes and figure, remember I told you about her?) with her boy-friend, and they were going out for coffee, and invited us to join them. It turns out that her boy-friend is a great friend of Tony's. Tony turns to me and says "O.K. with you, Elizabeth?", and before I knew what I was doing, I said yes that was fine with me, so off we go, and we're sitting there drinking coffee until quarter past eleven.

Tony started to walk home with me, but I got into a blue panic about what my parents would say when I arrived about forty minutes late. In the end I think I must have been crazy. I sat down by the side of the road and just refused to go any further, I couldn't bear the thought, in fact I just couldn't think straight. In the end, I told Tony to go home himself—he had to be home by midnight, and he had a two mile walk. He was so calm and understanding, and offered to explain to my parents, and take the blame himself, but by then I knew I would just have to face it alone. He wouldn't leave until he had persuaded me to start off down the street even though it was midnight—he phoned up his parents on the way home, apparently, and they were understanding about it, though I don't know if I'll ever be able to face them, or him, again.

I met my father in the next street—he was out with the car looking all over for me by this time. He was absolutely furious—he read me a lecture about what can happen to girls who act this way, and threatened never to let me go out at night again all term. Mummy was the worst, though. When I got home, she was crying, and hugging me, and the ash-tray was just full of all the stubs of the cigarettes she had smoked with worry. I felt really awful for what I'd done, and I tried to explain. Last night was just impossible, neither of them could listen to a word I said. Daddy was just as worried as Mummy, actually, but he shows it by getting furious. Anyway, this morning I talked things over with them, and tried to explain how it was. They were hurt when I told them about Annabel, I could see. Mummy tried to explain why I don't have as much money to spend on clothes as she does, and it made me feel about two inches tall. I wished I could die, honestly I did.

They were very nice about it in the end. I convinced them it really wasn't Tony's fault, and they aren't against him any more. I can't even think myself how it happened.

Love from your foolish friend,
Elizabeth.

Questions for Discussion

1 Have you formed a picture of the sort of girl Elizabeth is? Do you find her young for her age, or older than the average?

2 How do you feel about single-sex schools compared with mixed schools?

3 What do you think of Elizabeth's account of her 'flu attack? Was she as ill as she described, on the day she first became ill?

4 Is fifteen often a "horrid" year? Which year so far have you found the best, and the worst?

5 Can you explain Elizabeth's behaviour at 11.15 on Saturday night? Why did she make matters worse by sitting at the roadside instead of going home?

6 What do you think of Elizabeth's relationship with her parents?

7 Do you think Elizabeth and Tony will go out together again?

Trouble at the Youth Club

I

The Rev. Douglas Blake, a Youth Club Leader, and the Rev. John Smithers, the Diocesan Youth Officer, are talking together in Mr. Smithers' office.

SMITHERS: Look, Douglas, I'm not trying to interfere with your club arrangements but I think you should re-open as soon as you feel you can.

BLAKE: In principle, John, I agree with you, completely. You know that. But my position is really very difficult.

SMITHERS: I realize that, of course. But the longer you remain closed, the more difficult it will be to re-open. After all, you've put a great deal of time and effort into getting the club going at all. My colleagues and I, here in the office, have often commented on the tremendous progress you've made in less than twelve months.

BLAKE: It's not been long. In fact, we opened on October 1st last year. I remember that first night very well. Only two youngsters turned up—young Peter Hartridge and his sister Mary. Peter's made a good secretary, I must admit.

SMITHERS: Yes, a good lad. I was very impressed with him during my last visit.

BLAKE: Do you think I was wrong to close the club?

SMITHERS: Well, it's difficult to say. For a short time, surely. You've certainly had enough provocation. Do you have any idea of the cost of the damage yet?

BLAKE: Well, I've had an unofficial estimate for repairs and they are likely to come to well over a hundred pounds. Windows alone are likely to come to over forty pounds. And in some cases, it's not a matter of repairing. We shall have to replace completely.

SMITHERS: Yes, this kind of hooliganism can be very expensive.

BLAKE: Well, yes. But it's more than that, really. Somehow, these youngsters have got to learn that they can't just roam around being completely and violently anti-social without some sort of consequences to themselves. Somewhere along the line they've never been taught this.

SMITHERS: It's lack of any sense of responsibility, I suppose. Kids who just can't grow up. I'm on the side of the modern teenager. I wouldn't be in this job if I weren't, and neither would you. But something's gone wrong with the way they've been allowed to grow up.

BLAKE: But they're only hurting themselves. Can't they see this? Look at this club business; it's the first club ever in the village, the first real place for the kids to go to. And it was their own, something to build and make really worthwhile, and yet all they've done is wreck it.

SMITHERS: But not all of them have been involved in this.

BLAKE: No, not all. Some of them are O.K. And I feel it's wrong that they should suffer for the misdeeds of the rest. But what can I do? I don't really know who did all the damage. Probably more than one was in on it, bound to have been. No one lad could do all that damage.

SMITHERS: Oh, I don't know. I've seen some pretty wild ones in my time.

BLAKE: You think I should re-open soon then?

SMITHERS: Well, it's your decision. You have to live with the club and with the village, I don't. But if I were in your shoes. . . .

BLAKE: You don't think that they would see my going back on my first decision as a sign of weakness? I wouldn't mind for myself, but I think that it's important for the club, the community, for everybody.

SMITHERS: Look, Douglas, no-one could think of you as weak. Voluntary Service Overseas in the Pacific, a tough parish in the City before you came here, and a County rugger player. No, Douglas, no one is ever going to accuse you of being soft.

BLAKE: But if you've made a threat, don't you have to make it good? I said that we would stay closed for three months, and I don't see how I can really go back on that. I have to think of my total position in the village.

SMITHERS: Well, it's up to you.

BLAKE: And what if it all begins again when I re-open? What do I do then? It could be worse.

SMITHERS: It could be.

BLAKE: Perhaps I should have waited until I was more established in the village before tackling a club. I don't know. All I know really is that the youngsters were mooning about the village with nothing to do, getting into trouble because they were bored more often than not. I just couldn't stand by and let things rot like that.

SMITHERS: Well, Douglas, you've done your best. No man could have done more.

BLAKE: I'm not so sure. Oh, I know I've done the usual things—a coffee bar, games room, and not a bad football team on the way. I've tried discussions, debates even, and some role playing. I think we could raise a decent drama group with people like young Peter and his sister Mary.

SMITHERS: What about getting a few of them trying for the Duke of Edinburgh's Award?

BLAKE: I'd thought of that. There's a lot of things I'd like to do, given the chance.

SMITHERS: Well, all you've got to do is open up those doors again. You'd really made a first-class start, take it from an old hand.

BLAKE: Had I? Had I really? Perhaps I hadn't even begun.

II

Peter, Mary's brother, knocks on the door of her room that evening.

PETER: All right for me to come in, Mary?

MARY: That's O.K. All I have to do before I go to bed tonight is one History homework, one Physics, one Maths. and read all this novel.

PETER: Well, look, I know, but this is serious.

MARY: What is?

PETER: This club business.

MARY: Oh that. . . .

PETER: I'm sure that Blake is trying to do the right thing, but he can't close the club like this, not for three months.

MARY: Well, I don't know. From what I've seen of some of the goings on there I wonder whether he should have ever opened the place at all.

PETER: That's all very well, but where are all the kids going to go if there isn't such a place as the club?

MARY: Huh. You've got a vested interest, my dear brother. You're its one and only Secretary.

PETER: Well, there was nobody else.

MARY: You mean there was nobody else for Mr. Blake.

PETER: That's just not so. I was voted in and you jolly well know it.

MARY: Well ... yes ... but I'll bet that Odger and his gang wouldn't even have thought of you if it hadn't been for Blake.

PETER: Look, Mary ....

MARY: All right, all right. You were voted in *and* there was nobody else. But I think he was right to close the club. Somebody has to stop them wrecking the place.

PETER: But this isn't going to stop them. It'll be just the same when they come back, but this time it'll be worse. Some of these kids can carry a grudge for a long time.

MARY: Then what?

PETER: I think he's got the whole thing wrong. I think Blake should have thought about his action a lot more before he acted.

MARY: But he consulted you and the committee.

PETER: You mean he told us. He never asked us.

MARY: Looking at you and your committee, I don't blame him.

PETER: Mary, I'm serious. If he'd gone about the club in the right way from the beginning all this trouble would never arisen.

MARY: Nonsense.

PETER: It's not nonsense. It's just good sense. If he'd provided the right sort of activities from the beginning everything would have been O.K.

MARY: He's certainly done nothing for the girls. All he wants us for is to serve coke and coffee behind the bar and provide tea for the footballers on a Saturday afternoon. I was frozen at that last match.

PETER: Well, apart from the team and a bit of games equipment, just what has he done?

MARY: You're not asking me to defend him, are you?

PETER: No. But tell me what he's done?

MARY: Well, ... there's the coffee bar ... and ....

PETER: And?

106

MARY: Well, what about the discussion groups?

PETER. Oh, for heaven's sake, Mary, can you see people like Odger and gang ever discussing anything? What everybody wants is something to do.

MARY: Like tearing the place apart.

PETER: Oh, be serious, Mary. There are lots of things we could be doing. There's the Duke of Edinburgh's Award to begin with. And things like rock climbing at week ends and canoeing. Lots of really worthwhile things, which sound tough and are tough.

MARY: To that lot in the village? Oh, do come off it Peter. All that Odger and his lot want to do is roar round the place on their wretched motor-bikes.

PETER: Oh, I know, really. I sometimes wonder why Blake ever let them in. There was bound to be trouble from the start. Now if we only had a decent programme to offer. . . .

MARY: You'd still get somebody trying to take the place apart. They're like that. They just can't help it.

PETER: Well, maybe. But the trouble right now is that the membership is completely unbalanced and Odger and his gang can just take over. But if we had something to offer, really to offer, then I'm sure it could be different.

MARY: Well, why don't you tell him?

PETER: Oh, he'd never listen to me. It would be like telling a master at school how to do his job.

MARY: And everyone knows you can't tell them anything. Oh, come on Peter, he's really not all that bad. He'd take it from you.

PETER: I'm not so sure. I know he often makes out that he's all friendly and chummy. But I don't think he ever listens to anything really. He's an idealist and idealists never listen to anybody.

MARY: Well, look, you came in here asking for my advice, and I've given it to you.

PETER: Well, yes, I know, but . . . .

MARY: Look, you are the Secretary, aren't you? So you've got to tell him. But don't think you're going to solve the world's problems.

PETER: I'm not trying to solve the world's problems. I just want the club to open again, but with a decent programme this time and a membership that's really right.

MARY: Well, you'd better get started. Personally, I just have to finish this homework before I go to bed tonight . . . .

Questions for Discussion

1 Do you know how the committee of the Youth Club is normally chosen and how it works?

2 Why do young people join youth clubs and similar voluntary organizations (e.g. the Scouts, the Girl Guides, the Cadet Forces, the Brigade, etc.)? If you are a member of one of these groups, why did you join?

3 If you are not a member of a youth group, were there any special reasons why you decided not to join or which in some way prevented you from joining a group?

4 What are the kinds of things (activities, belonging to a group, etc.) which would attract you to a youth group?

5 What do you think were some of the problems facing the Rev. Blake's Youth Club?

6 If you were in Peter's shoes, what would you do?

7 Suppose you were in the position of the Rev. Blake. What would you do?

8 You have heard the Rev. Blake's story of his troubles, and Peter's. Now imagine Odger talking about the club to one or two of his own "gang," as Peter and Mary call them. You could either "role-play" this conversation, or write out a short piece of dialogue.

9 You may not agree with Blake's and Smithers' assumptions about "modern youth," but you will probably agree that in every generation some people are less responsible

than others. Are there any ways in which people can be helped to develop a better sense of responsibility?

He Cut His Wrists

Michael Jones was feeling fairly cheerful as he climbed on to the school bus on Friday afternoon, at the end of a week of hard work revising for exams. He was one of the last to get off the bus, as he lived out in a small village some distance from the school, and by the time he arrived home it was already beginning to get dark.

Michael lived with his father. His aunt, Aunt Sue, came in from time to time, to help out with practical details of running a home which neither Michael nor his father found easy. Mr. Jones was a research chemist in the large chemical fibre company nearby, and Michael enjoyed the rare occasions when he and his father talked together about the latter's work.

Michael could not remember his mother. She had gone away with another man, and been divorced by his father, when Michael was only two and a half. There were no pictures of her left openly around in the house, but Michael had seen snapshots of her at his grandparents' house. He used to run into the garden with them when he was small, and ask the smiling face what he had done to make her run away. He had once heard his father say that he had been a difficult, crying child, and his mother had run away to escape mother-hood as much as to be with her "very ordinary" friend.

Aunt Sue, and a succession of housekeepers, had done all that had seemed necessary to fill a mother's place for Michael, and he loved his father very dearly. Often he found himself with the thought that he was lucky to have his clever father all to himself, but then he would think how selfish and cruel that thought was. Most of the time, he had to admit, he was really a very happy person. Michael excelled at school work, and easily reached top position in his class in the weekly lists every time. In spite of this, no-one seemed to resent his success, because no matter how well he did, he himself was never satisfied, and worked harder and harder, striving for the sort of perfection he felt he must achieve.

Michael's schoolfriends, indeed, often said that at sixteen he was more like an old man than another boy. He had a rather heavy humour, towards which, for some reason, they were always tolerant. He had a way of talking in clichés about "being grateful for the good things in life," and "looking back over my life I feel I have much to be thankful for." In spite of this, most of his associates liked him well enough. He was "The Brain" to them all, but he was unfailingly polite and ready to help other people with thorny problems in homework or exam. revision.

Michael was small for his age, but the girls who knew him agreed privately that he was very good-looking—not that he ever showed any interest in any of them. When he was twelve, he had had a close friendship with a girl from the same village, and they had held hands on the bus going home, written notes to each other to be left in the hollow of a tree, and vowed to get married as soon as they legally could. After a blissful summer in this happy state, however, the girl had moved away far beyond his reach, and he had felt that his suffering was greater than he could bear.

He was remembering her as he walked home from the bus, because one of the girls had heard from her, and so she had been the topic for discussion during the early part of the journey. As he walked along thinking of her, Michael realized that one of what he personally described to himself as his "Black Moods" was coming over him. These moods were his own private nightmare, with him since the age of fourteen, and for two years he had been unexpectedly hit by overwhelming despair perhaps once every three or four weeks, in phases that lasted perhaps two days, perhaps only twelve hours. Some small event, or a conversation, would bring on these moods, in the midst of a normal day, when he was feeling as cheerful as usual.

What Michael hated most about the "Black Moods" was the way in which they engulfed everything. He used to make a conscious effort to avoid thinking about particularly happy occasions or events while the mood was on, because everything that passed through his mind at these times seemed to be permanently tainted by the blackness, so that he never saw it in the same way again. There was no way to look for comfort or relief while the mood was on him—literally everything seemed utterly grey and meaningless, dust and ashes, no goal seemed worth striving for, no triumph worth his pride.

Michael fought the mood with logic as he walked up the path to his home. I'm hungry, I'm worried about exams, I'm upset at remembering Jeannie and the way she went away, that's all, he told himself. Once I've eaten, I'll be fine.

His mood did not much improve during a rather silent supper of cheese and soup with his father. He opened his books, up in his room after supper, and found the same feeling of hollowness assailing him again. What, a voice inside him asked, is all this work for? Will it mean anything if I get all the exam. honours in the world?

Michael heard his father's footsteps coming up the stairs.

"Michael, I've something I want to ask you about," his father began. "You're sixteen now, more than capable of looking after yourself, I know. We've rubbed along together, the two of us, and I'm jolly glad we've managed as well as we have. The thing is this. I've been offered a chance to go over to the States for six months, for the firm. It'll be a marvellous chance to see the work they're doing there in my field, and I'll love meeting the men I've only known through correspondence about work problems before. The trouble is, it means leaving you here on your own. I realize it's just when "O" levels come along, though I'll be back before they start, but Aunt Sue will be just three doors away all the time —in fact you can move in with her if you wish, she says. What do you say? Can you cope without me for that long? If you say no, I won't go. I've explained that to the director."

Michael felt a sudden twist inside him. Outwardly, however, he grinned at once, and said how marvellous, wasn't that splendid? And of course he'd manage, he'd be all right alone, he'd managed before often enough for the odd day or two. No problem.

They talked a few minutes more, and Michael could see that his father was longing to take this opportunity as soon as possible. Inside him, though, there was a rising tide of nausea and physical panic. As soon as he could, he ended the conversation and rushed along to the bathroom. Clutching the washbasin sides, he caught sight of himself in the mirror. "I hate you, hate you, hate you," he screamed at his image silently and internally. "You're no good, no good to anyone. Why, oh why, do I have to live with you?"

In a choking rage, he smashed his fist into the mirror. He was shaking uncontrollably, and he felt as if a red cloud was over his brain, making thought impossible. He heard himself sob aloud as he picked up one of the jagged pieces of the mirror, and he slashed violently and clumsily, again and again, at his left wrist, then his right.

Fortunately, not too much time elapsed before Mr. Jones realized something was wrong, and Michael was taken to hospital, and recovered. A week later, he insisted on returning to school.

Questions for Discussion
1 What other kinds of unhappy family circumstances might produce a boy with Michael's extreme feelings?

112

2 How much are Michael's problems only likely to be experienced by very clever boys and girls?

3 What sort of reasons do drive people to attempt suicide?

4 How do you think Michael's father would feel, when he realized what Michael had done?

5 Suicide is often described as a cowardly death. Do you agree?

6 Could Michael be helped now by the way his friends at school behave towards him?

7 Almost all quite normal people have occasional moments when they think about suicide. What reasons do almost all of us have for rejecting the idea as totally absurd? List some of your very good reasons for enjoying life.

Selected Bibliography

FAMILY RELATIONSHIPS

FLETCHER, R. *The Family and Marriage in Britain.* Harmondsworth. Rev. ed. Penguin, 1966.

GOODE, W. J. *The Family.* New York: Prentice-Hall, 1964.

KLEIN, J. *Samples from English Cultures.* London: Routledge & Kegan Paul, 1965.

MUSGROVE, F. *Youth and the Social Order.* London: Routledge, 1964.

GROUP RELATIONSHIPS

HARGREAVES, D. *Social Relations in the Secondary School.* London: Routledge & Kegan Paul, 1967.

JACKSON, B. *Streaming: An Education System in Miniature.* London: Routledge & Kegan Paul, 1964.

OTTAWAY, A. K. C. *Learning through Group Experience.* London: Routledge & Kegan Paul, 1966.

SHERIF, M., and C. W. *Reference Groups: Exploration in Conformity and Deviation.* New York: Harper & Row, 1964.

BOY-GIRL RELATIONSHIPS

ALDERSON, C. *Magazines Teenagers Read.* Oxford: Pergamon, 1968.

EPPEL, E. M., & EPPEL, M. *Adolescents and Morality.* London: Routledge & Kegan Paul, 1966.

HEMMING, J. *Problems of Adolescent Girls.* London: Heinemann, 1960.

SCHOFIELD, M. *Adolescents and Sexual Behaviour.* London: Longmans, 1965.

PERRY, P. *Your Guide to the Opposite Sex.* London: Pitman, 1970.

INTO WORK

CARTER, M. *Into Work*. Harmondsworth: Pelican (Penguin Books), 1966.

MACKENZIE, R. F. *Escape from the Classroom*. London: Collins, 1965.

VENESS, T. *School Leavers*. London: Methuen, 1962.

Half Our Future. A Report of the Central Advisory Council for Education (England): H.M.S.O., 1963.

DEVIANT BEHAVIOUR

FYVEL, T. R. *The Insecure Offenders*. London: Chatto & Windus, 1961.

HECKINGER, G. & F. *Teenage Tyranny*. London: Duckworth, 1965.

MAYS, J. B. *The Young Pretenders*. London: Michael Joseph, 1965.

MORSE, M. *The Unattached*. Harmondsworth: Pelican (Penguin Books), 1965.

DEVELOPMENT CAN BE PAINFUL

ERIKSON, E. H. *Youth: Change & Challenge*. New York: Basic Books, 1963.

ERIKSON, E. H. *Childhood and Society*. New York: Norton, 1950.

HADFIELD, J. A. *Childhood and Adolescence*. Harmondsworth: Pelican (Penguin Books), 1962.

LOUKES, H. *Teenage Religion*. London: S. C. M., 1961.

WILSON, J., WILLIAMS, N., & SUGARMAN, B. *Introduction to Moral Education*. Harmondsworth: Pelican (Penguin Books), 1967.